D. H. LAWRENCE
The Phoenix and the Flame

D. H. LAWRENCE

The Phoenix and the Flame

for John, with best wishes. from Geoffrey

Geoffrey Trease

The phoenix renews her youth
only when she is burnt, burnt alive ....

   D. H. Lawrence, LAST POEMS

Macmillan

© Geoffrey Trease 1973

SBN   333   13766   3

First published 1973 by
MACMILLAN LONDON LIMITED
London and Basingstoke
Associated companies in New York
Dublin Melbourne Johannesburg and Madras

Printed in Great Britain by
NORTHUMBERLAND PRESS LIMITED
Gateshead

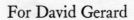
For David Gerard

Contents

List of Illustrations

Acknowledgments

This account of D. H. Lawrence's life – and above all the authentic word-by-word dialogue, all based on the first-hand recollection of people present at the time – has been reconstructed from the countless biographies and memoirs among which the author is particularly and deeply indebted to the following: *The Intelligent Heart* by Harry T. Moore; *D. H. Lawrence, A Composite Biography* edited by Edward Nehls; *D. H. Lawrence, A Personal Record* by 'E. T.'; *Lawrence in Love: Letters from D. H. Lawrence to Louie Burrows* edited by James T. Boulton; and *Not I, But the Wind* ... by Frieda Lawrence. Special thanks are due to Professor Boulton for lending me the typescript, before publication, of an article, 'Memories of D. H. Lawrence' by the late Professor J. D. Chambers, and to the editors of *Renaissance and Modern Studies* (University of Nottingham) for permission to quote from it.

For permission to reprint extracts from the work of D. H. Lawrence acknowledgment is made to Messrs Laurence Pollinger Ltd, the Estate of the late Mrs Frieda Lawrence, and to Messrs William Heinemann Ltd.

The author is much indebted to the City Librarian of Nottingham, Mr Paul Sykes, and Miss Lucy Edwards of the Local History Department for their courtesy and assistance; to a former member of the staff, Mr George Roberts, unfailingly helpful in the quest for illustrations; and to the former City Librarian, Mr David Gerard, who so kindly read the typescript and placed his deep knowledge of D. H. Lawrence's life and work at the author's disposal.

For permission to reproduce the various illustrations acknowledgments are due as follows: for the picture of Lawrence at 21, to the Cambridge University Press. For the pictures of Lawrence in 1913, and of Frieda von Richthofen, to the University of Wisconsin and Mrs Barbara Weekley Barr. For the picture of Louie Burrows to Professor James T. Boulton, for that of Helen Corke to the University of Texas Press, for the Lawrence family group, the colliery scene, and the photograph of the bust of Lawrence by Jo Davidson, to Laurence Pollinger Ltd. For the picture of Jessie Chambers and the view of Haggs Farm to Nottingham Public Libraries and the estate of J. D. Chambers. For the picture of Dorothy Brett, to the Hon. Dorothy Brett. For the pictures of Katherine Mansfield and Middleton Murry to David Higham Associates Ltd. The view from Lawrence's cabin near Taos and the picture of Mabel Dodge are by courtesy of the Humanities Research Center, the University of Texas. The still from the film *The Virgin and the Gypsy* is by courtesy of London Screen Enterprises Ltd and the Simkins Partnership. The picture of Fontana Vecchia is from a photograph by Mrs Geoffrey Trease. With the exception of the four last mentioned, all photographs have been supplied by the City of Nottingham Public Libraries.

AUTHOR'S NOTE

I never met D. H. Lawrence. We walked the same streets of that English Midland city and the same school corridors, we faced some of the same teachers in the same old classrooms. But he was twenty-four years ahead of me, and by the time I was growing up he seldom, if ever, was seen in Nottingham.

I knew of him, of course. He figured in newspaper headlines. He was famous. He wrote dirty books, it was said, and painted filthy pictures. The police had seized some of both. What else could you expect, my elders muttered, of a wild young scoundrel with a beard who had run off with another man's wife?

Then one day in London when I was twenty, walking along Fleet Street, I saw another headline in the window of a newspaper office: Lawrence was dead. On an impulse I turned into a bookshop and bought one of his novels, *Sons and Lovers*. Reading it that night, I was transported to my native city and its surrounding countryside. I caught the very speech I had heard around me in childhood.

'"Ask him if the London train's come," said Paul ...

"I'm not," said Annie. "You be quiet – he might send us off."'

Pure Nottingham, I thought, the girl's reply.

There was more to it than homesickness, more to it than local pride. I fell under the spell of what is now recognised to be one of the most important English novels of the early twentieth century. Soon I was dashing off an obituary notice for my old school magazine. I have just re-read, for the first time, what I wrote more than forty years ago:

'To most members of the School his name is probably unknown or at best a byword when the censorship is discussed. Lawrence's work is not likely to interest the average boy.' (I was wrong there, I think, and certainly wrong so far as the modern boy is concerned, and the reason I gave sounds odd today.) 'He [Lawrence] sees life as something very serious and cruel and devoid of humour ... Nevertheless, the critics are agreed that he was a great artist, and that the best of his work, both poems and fiction, will last. The School will be proud of her rebellious son long after those more convention-ally honoured are forgotten.'

Conventional honours would not have appealed to Law-rence. He would have disdained memorial tablets or prizes, though as a boy he had won prizes himself. But eighteen months after his death I collected signatures for a letter, also published in the school magazine, suggesting that a tree, to be known as Lawrence's Tree, might be planted in the grounds and that 'many men distinguished in litera-ture would be only too glad to come down to plant it with appropriate ceremony'. The proposal fell flat as a dead fish. A member of the staff warned me, 'You'll get nowhere so long as So-and-so is Second Master – he's a personal friend of Professor Weekley.' I understood then how hopeless my plan was. For the one-time Mrs Weekley had for many years been Mrs Lawrence.

Once roused, my interest in Lawrence never died. And now that his books are studied in schools there seems a need for a simple telling of his stormy life-story – a good story in itself, and essential to the understanding of his ideas, which once shocked the world but have now in many respects become part of our everyday lives.

Possibly it is a good thing that I never met him. For in the years following his death, books fairly cascaded from the publishers. Every one who had been his friend or enemy (and most had been both at different times) wrote what he claimed to be *the* book on Lawrence. All those books, though they preserved a wealth of facts, were to some extent distorted by love, hatred, jealousy, resentment or revenge. It was sometimes hard to believe that they were describing the same person. So there is something to be said for writing calmly about Lawrence, like any other character in history.

It is, however, an advantage to have known some of the places and people Lawrence knew in his formative years – the woods and fields of Nottinghamshire, the mining villages as they were in his time, the black-faced colliers squatting against the wall, the city with its colourful market-stalls and river steamers and Castle Rock depicted in his early novels, the schoolmasters, Nipper and Jumbo and the rest, who taught him as they afterwards taught me. Many of the later scenes are also known to me at first-hand – Zennor on the wild Cornish cliffs, where the detectives searched Lawrence's cottage on suspicion that he was a German spy, and the old Sicilian farmhouse of Fontana Vecchia, where he met a snake at the water-trough and wrote one of his best-known poems, and Mayrhofen in the Austrian Tyrol, and countless other places in Britain or abroad that figure in his restless odyssey.

I am grateful too to have had brief encounters, while they were still alive, with several people besides his schoolmasters, who figured in important early episodes in his story – the unfortunate Ernest Weekley, David Chambers, youngest of the family Lawrence used to visit at Haggs Farm, and his sister, Jessie, the 'Miriam' of *Sons and Lovers*. It is with Jessie's first meeting with Lawrence – he fifteen, she fourteen – described by her, thirty-four years afterwards, that the story may most fittingly begin.

1   THE MINER'S SON

Tea was finished. The farmhouse parlour was stuffy in the early summer heat. They went outside, the two mothers deep in their own talk. The boy and girl were left to themselves, strangers, awkward, thrown together.

The farm was an out-of-the-way place. It stood on a hill, looking across to massed woodlands and a gleam of water. She took him through the stackyard into a field and he stood silent, drinking in the view.

She was the nervous one. It was her home, but even so she felt at a disadvantage. This boy, she knew, was clever. He went to the High School in the city, ten miles away. He wore the striped trousers, short jacket and wide starched collar that such schools had copied from Eton. He knew French and German.

She herself had been taken away from school six months before. She was bitter about it, conscious that she was uneducated, resentful because she loved books. At this moment she was angry because the boy seemed to think she was not worth talking to. He went on gazing at the distant woods, stand-offish, stiff as his own Eton collar.

She broke the silence. 'How old are you?'

Now he glanced at her. 'Fifteen.'

'I thought so.' She tried to soften her bluntness. 'I'm fourteen.' As he made no effort to develop the conversation she asked: 'You go to school?'

'Yes, to the High.'

Silence again. Irritated, she tried another tack. 'I don't care for the name Bertie. It's a girlish name. Do they call you Bertie at school?'

'No, of course not. They call me Lawrence.'

'That's nicer, I think. I'd rather call you Lawrence.'

This time there was more animation in his reply. 'Do call me Lawrence. I'd like it better.'

Contact had been made.

That scene took place in 1901. The world stood on the threshold of the twentieth century. Britain was especially conscious of changes in the air, for the great Queen Victoria had died only a few months before, after reigning so long that hardly any one alive could remember when there had been a king. Change was in the air for Lawrence too. He was in his last term at school and would soon be looking for a job. And he had just met, on that afternoon at Haggs Farm, the girl who was to play a central role in his life over the next few years.

To understand that silent schoolboy it is necessary to go back to the beginning.

David Herbert Richards Lawrence was born at Eastwood, a little mining town in Nottinghamshire, on September 11, 1885. He was thus in date a 'Victorian', and grew up in that atmosphere of outward respectability, convention and taboo, that is usually associated with the

18

Victorian age. He was to revolt violently against it, but he never quite shook off its influence.

His mother, who so dominated his early life, was a true Victorian, genteel, a prim chapel-goer. Her father had been a dockyard engineer in Kent. She herself had been a teacher. She read, even wrote a little, had offered poems unsuccessfully to magazines. She hated the rough working class world into which she had married. She felt superior to her neighbours. She was fiercely determined that her sons should get on. She corrected them if they spoke the dialect they heard from their schoolmates and from their own father.

Mr Lawrence was entirely different. He had no use for 'fancy' talk and 'fancy' manners. He was a butty in the mines, a sort of working sub-contractor, recruiting his own small gang to hew coal from a particular section or stall. He had met his future wife in Nottingham, for, though she had grown up in the south, her family like his was rooted in that town. They were in fact connected by marriage, her uncle being married to his aunt, and their first encounter was at a Christmas party.

Arthur Lawrence had a way with him – an infectious laugh, merry blue eyes, ruddy cheeks, and a curly black beard. Lydia was then twenty-three and had already suffered a disappointment in love. The young man's vitality charmed her. They were married in Nottingham and she woke up to reality only when they set up their first home in the mining area outside. She had been courted by a gay young 'contractor' as he called himself, well scrubbed, clad in his best suit. Now she found herself sharing house and bed with a workman who came home black from the pit and took his bath shameless before the kitchen fire – a man who no longer checked his coarse speech, who sometimes drank too much with his mates, and, when she nagged him with her sharp teacher's tongue, only stayed out longer and drank more.

They lived at several different places in the mining area north and west of Nottingham. It was the ancient Sherwood Forest country, and some of the belts of beautiful woodland remained, as they still do. But mostly it was a mixed landscape of farmland, big mansions set in ornamental grounds and tree-dotted pastures, and ugly straggling colliery villages. The headstocks rose blackly against the sky with the great wheels that sent the cages down into the depths below. Drab pyramids of 'spoil' – the waste earth excavated from the workings – dominated the scene. A network of railway lines covered the district. Endless trains of coal-trucks clattered and squealed. Locomotives belched trails of gritty smoke.

Industrial development was going full blast. Bigger companies were taking over the shallow, small-scale mines that had existed for centuries. New and deeper shafts were being sunk, more and more coal gouged out of the earth. No one talked of 'pollution' then. Few people questioned that 'progress' was a good thing – and they were dismissed as eccentric. Yet from his early years D. H. Lawrence hated what he saw modern industry doing to the land and people around him. That hatred became one of the most powerful themes in his books.

Arthur and Lydia Lawrence had five children. George and Ernest came first, then Emily. Bert was the fourth, born in a small red-brick house at the corner of Victoria Street, Eastwood. Earlier, his mother had turned the front room into a shop. She had filled the window with linen and the cheap machine-made lace which the Nottingham factories sent out all over the world. But as more children were born she gave up this effort to make extra money and to raise herself above the level of the neighbours.

From the day he was born Bert showed that frailty which dogged him throughout his life and played such an important part in determining the way his mind and character developed. Indeed, that life was nearly cut short by bronchitis when he was only two weeks old. His mother, pushing his pram along the main street, prophesied gloomily to the friends she met that she did not expect him to get through the winter. He did, but he was a skinny little child, unable to hold his own in rough games with other boys. Clearly he would never match his elder brother, Ernest, who was a keen athlete and swimmer.

In 1887, when Mrs Lawrence bore her last child, Ada, the family moved a short distance to the Breach, the name given to a group of cottages built by the mining company to house its workmen. In *Sons and Lovers* this location appears as 'the Bottoms'. Lawrence was never interested in inventing – almost everything in his books is taken from the actual scenes, characters and incidents of his own life, often used more than once, and with little effort to disguise or vary them. When studying his novels one has to refer continually to his biography. One has to be watchful, however, for those important occasions when Lawrence, while seeming to reproduce something faithfully from his own experience, has distorted the truth to suit his prejudice.

Mrs Lawrence hated the Breach – she hated a lot of things and had a permanent grievance against Life. She was an emphatic little woman, her face full of animation, her head bobbing with vehemence as she stated her views. She resented having to live among people whom she looked down on as uncouth and uneducated.

So, after four years, the family moved again, up the hill to Walker Street, which was their home for the rest of Bert's childhood. From this higher position one could look across the drab slate roofs below, past the chimneys with their skeins of smoke, to a skyline of green woods and hills beyond. 'I lived in that house from the age of six to eighteen,' he once told a friend with emotion. 'I know that view better than any in the world.'

Walker Street itself was unlovely enough. But an ash tree raised its branches bravely on the opposite side of the street, and in the back-yard, on a tiny patch of soil between clothes-line and ash-pit, Mrs Lawrence scattered some mixed flower-seeds. When they came up, she disparaged them and called the patch a wilderness, but Bert was delighted with them, hopping with excitement as he showed the flowers to callers and cried in his shrill voice, 'I think they're ever so nice, don't you?'

When he was old enough he followed his elder brothers and sister to the Beauvale Board School a short walk away. Like many a child before and after, he wept bitterly on that first morning. Instinctively, as throughout his life, he shied away from the confines of an institution. Even his identity seemed to be taken away. The fierce-looking bearded head teacher, Mr Whitehead – known to the children as 'the Gaffer', or boss – wanted to call him 'David', because that was his first name in the register. But David Herbert Lawrence was 'Bert' or 'Bertie' at home (though he came to dislike his second name as well) and he refused to answer to 'David'. The Gaffer invoked the authority of the Bible. 'David', he thundered, 'was the name of a great and good man!' The little boy glowered. It might be all right for the Psalmist, but it was not *his* name. His career of rebellion had begun.

He had a hard time in the playground, too. He had never been strong enough for boys' games, he had no aptitude for them and no interest. Inevitably he found that he had more in common with the girls. The boys teased him for this and chanted behind him in the street:

'Dicky Dicky Denches
Plays with the wenches!'

He walked on, ignoring them. But already, it is easy to
see now, another traceable thread began to be woven into
the fabric of his life, the sense that he was different and,
because he was different, would be the object of persecution by the ignorant.

His mother's snobbery lent him courage. It helped him
to build up a contempt for his persecutors, a conviction
that he was right, they wrong. And his mother's respect
for education, as a former teacher herself, helped him to
bear the ordeal of those schooldays. He wanted to do
well, to please her. He gritted his teeth and persevered.
In time the Gaffer perceived that he had a bright pupil
and he began to coach him for a scholarship to the High
School in Nottingham.

At home, on Saturday mornings, Bert helped his adored
mother with household jobs which in other mining
families were scornfully left to the girls. May Chambers,
Jessie's elder sister, visited his home before the days at
Haggs Farm. Long afterwards she remembered finding
him, as a ten-year-old, 'cleaning boots or knives and forks,
with an apron tied under his armpits, a smudge on his
face, and his thick, fine hair rumpled'. A few years later
he might still have been seen scrubbing the floor or
blackleading the grate. Much later still, as a married man,
it was he who was the domesticated one and had to do the
cooking until his wife could learn the art. But in 1900 –
and indeed for almost another half century, until the
second World War had broken down such conventions –
a boy or a man who helped with 'women's work' was
apt to be ridiculed, and nowhere more than among the
tough manual workers.

Mrs Lawrence prided herself on keeping a genteel home

23

in which books were read (she especially enjoyed Walter Scott) and the Congregational minister could be offered tea. Bert had to attend service regularly, as well as Sunday School, Christian Endeavour, and the children's anti-liquor organisation, the Band of Hope.

It was only in his late teens that he revolted against all this compulsory religion. He liked the Gothic chapel with its tall spire and colour-washed interior. It provided some beauty and grandeur in that squalid environment. The hymns, too, were not sentimental but rousing, with plenty of fight in them. He remembered those hymns as long as he lived. And deep in his consciousness he absorbed the prose of the Bible, which became the basis for his own command of language.

Mr Lawrence cared less for the chapel. It was against drink, while he was very much *for* drink, and was more at ease in a public bar. If he came home, grimy and ex-hausted after a hard day, he was not pleased to find the best tea-service set out on a dainty cloth in the parlour and his wife exchanging refined conversation with the min-ister. He would react by deliberately uncouth behaviour. If he could drive away these unwanted visitors by shock-ing them, so much the better.

Thus there was unceasing strife between the parents, another influence that left an indelible mark on the boy's character and coloured his view of the relationship be-tween the sexes. In that strife he was always on his mother's side. May Chambers observed his manner when she went to tea, and she was so embarrassed that she could scarcely swallow her food. When Mr Lawrence came in from the pit, and sat down to the dinner kept hot for him, the boy was instantly transformed.

'I tried to find a word to fit Bert's attitude,' the girl recalled, 'and discovered it was *vengeful*. He was totally unlike the boy who lit up the rather drab room with a

24

dancing light like a sunbeam. He seemed to gather the gloom of the back yard into his being and crouch among the shabbiness like something sinister.' He seemed, she went on, 'to send out jagged waves of hate and loathing that made me shudder'.

She could see nothing in his father's behaviour to justify this. Mr Lawrence talked affably as he ate. He listened to the chatter of his youngest child, Ada, and asked May to 'come and see us again before long'. But while he remained in the house Bert sat silently hunched up on the sofa beside his mother. When his father went out there was another transformation. He became a lively boy again.

This father-and-son tension, now recognised as natural and within reason harmless, a phenomenon born of human relationships, was in Lawrence's case carried to extremes. He could not please his mother without hating his father. When he grew up he realised, like many other sons, that there were two sides to the coin. He told friends that he had given an unfair picture of his father in *Sons and Lovers*, where he is depicted as drinking and lying, 'often a poltroon, sometimes a knave', 'blab-mouthed, a tongue-wagger', who 'scarcely spared the children an extra penny or bought them a pound of apples', and a bully who, 'while the baby was still tiny', could hit him with 'the hard hands of the collier'. Lawrence confessed that he 'felt like rewriting' the novel, but he never did so.

In that book the contrast between the parents is exaggerated. The miner's uncouthness is emphasised to set off his wife's social superiority. It is one of the stock themes in Lawrence's work, recurring again and again, the union of the virile, primitive, uneducated man with a more cultured woman. As fiction the contrast is dramatically effective. As a barely disguised representation of his own parents it is unjustified.

They did not come from different classes. Mr Lawrence's father had been a tailor, who had married the daughter of a Nottingham silk and lace manufacturer. One of Mrs Lawrence's grandfathers had also been a lace manufacturer in that town.

Mr Lawrence's becoming a miner, instead of a tailor, had happened naturally enough, for his father had set up his business in Brinsley, the next colliery village to Eastwood, and the basis of his trade was the supply of working clothes. Arthur John Lawrence, when he grew up, simply went down the pit with the other local lads instead of joining his father with scissors and sewing machine.

He became a skilled workman, respected alike by his mates and by his employers, who always turned to him when some tricky job presented itself. He had been in Nottingham, helping to sink a new shaft on the outskirts of the town, when he had had his first ill-fated encounter with his future wife. True, he drank – how many men did not, in that hard-working community, when every day they risked death underground, and had little choice of relaxation when they came to the surface again? Mrs Lawrence, with her hatred of alcohol, made the most of his weakness, but it was she who drove him out of the kitchen and into the public bar.

It was not uncommon for the miners' wives or even the children to go to the colliery office for their wages. Mrs Lawrence was not the woman to stand in that line with her neighbours, and it fell to her boys to perform the errand. When Bert grew old enough to be sent, he detested the teasing of the cashier. 'Ho, lad, where's your pa? Too drunk to collect the pay himself?' It was a cruel jibe, probably without basis in fact, certainly unforgivable to aim at a sensitive child, and it served to strengthen Bert's faith that his mother was right in all she said.

Yet Mr Lawrence was not the beery, black-faced animal

she made him out to be. He was, for example, an expert dancer. Even Bert admitted that, and revealed an unusual pride in his father's skill. 'I don't know anybody else's father who knows the science about dancing, do you?' he once asked his young friends at Haggs Farm. 'Some can dance, of course, but Father knows how to teach it.' And when they complained that the farm kitchen was too small for such a crowd, he quoted his father against them: 'Father says you should be able to dance on a threepenny bit. Come on, now, and everybody sing.'

It would be a mistake to picture that childhood as all tension, family quarrels and unhappiness. When the father was out, as he mostly was, the atmosphere was gay enough. Mrs Lawrence gave her children love – many would say, too much love. She entered keenly into their interests. She prided herself on keeping young that way.

Outside the house there was liveliness too. Twice a year the travelling fairs set up their booths and merry-go-rounds outside the town. There were companies of actors, presenting Shakespearean tragedy and gory melodrama in a tent. There were popular concerts and 'penny readings', when the works of Dickens or some other favourite author were read to appreciative audiences. Television, radio and even the cinema were still to be invented. People enjoyed themselves none the less – indeed perhaps the more, since these simple amusements drew them out of their homes and fused them into a warm neighbourly mass.

Then there were the quieter pleasures of the country. The colliery villages might themselves be drab, but they were so interlaced with their rural surroundings that one was never far from hayfields and hawthorn hedges. Usually on Saturdays Bert and his sisters used to take the footpath to Brinsley to visit their grandfather, the old tailor, and he would pick apples for them. At the same time of year they would go blackberrying. George

Lawrence used to recall his little brother's delicacy. 'I've carried him on my shoulder for miles.' So, from his earliest years, Bert absorbed the sights and sounds and smells of the countryside, which helped him to become one of the supreme descriptive writers to portray the English scene. He began to acquire, too, his keenly sympathetic eye for wild creatures.

This observation was not restricted to his consciously literary work. He could not help pouring the same richness into private letters. Thus, he wrote to Katherine Mansfield from Derbyshire in February, 1919: 'Yesterday I went out for a real walk ... I climbed with my niece to the bare top of the hills. Wonderful it is to see the footmarks on the snow – beautiful ropes of rabbit prints, trailing away over the brows; heavy hare marks; a fox, so sharp and dainty, going over the wall; birds with two feet that hop; very splendid straight advance of a pheasant; wood-pigeons that are clumsy and move in flocks; splendid little leaping marks of weasels, coming along like a necklace chain of berries; odd little filigree of the field-mice; the trail of a mole – it is astonishing what a world of wild creatures one feels round one, on the hills in the snow.'

In his poems he is outstanding in his depiction of animals and birds, insects and reptiles – a bat in his room in Florence, blundering round 'with a twitchy, nervous, intolerable flight', or a majestic golden snake sipping from the water-trough in Sicily, or a dead mountain lion in New Mexico, 'a long, long slim cat' with

Her round, bright face, bright as frost.
Her round, fine-fashioned head, with two dead ears;
And stripes in the brilliant frost of her face, sharp,
    fine dark rays,
Dark, keen, fine rays in the brilliant frost of her face.
Beautiful dead eyes.

Nearly always it was the wild things. His mother never encouraged the children to mar her tidy home by keeping pets.

Mrs Lawrence kept one objective clear before her eyes: her boys were not going to do as other Eastwood boys did, and follow their father into the mines. George she apprenticed to an uncle in Nottingham who was a picture-framer. George left home before he was ten and thereafter, for all the pangs of separation from him, she knew he was safe from the pit. Ernest was brighter at school – she found him an office job and he went from strength to strength, blossoming out at twenty-one as clerk in a London shipping firm, in all the late-Victorian splendour of top hat and frock coat, an object of both awe and ridicule when he came home to Eastwood.

Bert also must do well. At least his frail physique removed any possibility of the pit. He was not fond of school, but she was sure that he could equal Ernest if he stuck to his books. Disregarding the headaches he complained of, she urged him on. She had the full co-operation of Gaffer Whitehead, who, though stern and handy with the cane, knew a bright boy when he saw one.

It was less than thirty years since education had been made compulsory in England, and for the masses it was still of a very elementary type. Parents wanting more had to pay fees for better schools. There was so much poverty that most working class children had to start earning wages as soon as possible.

There had been started, however, a system of scholarships. Clever children could take an examination and win free places at the grammar schools mainly filled with fee-payers from the middle class. If Bert could win a Nottinghamshire County scholarship before he was thirteen, he could go to the High School in the city, learn French, wear an Eton collar and become a gentleman.

Mrs Lawrence determined that he should do just that. She worked hard at it, the Gaffer worked too, and so presumably did her obedient son. In that summer of 1898, competing against boys from a wide area, D. H. Lawrence of Beauvale Board School was listed among the winners.

It should have been wonderful – a triumph for his mother's social ambitions, a door of opportunity opening before an intelligent and interested boy.

The High School, as it had recently been renamed, was an ancient institution, founded in 1513, 'evermore to endure', so ran King Henry the Eighth's licence, 'for the education, teaching and instruction of boys in good manners and literature'.

It had endured by then for almost four centuries. It had known its ups and downs, but of late it had been steadily on the upgrade. A vigorous headmaster had doubled the numbers, which, in the year Bert Lawrence entered, stood at 381, the highest ever known.

It had moved in mid-Victorian times to impressive new buildings on a steep sandstone ridge overlooking the town. Trudging up from the railway station each morning, Bert could see it from afar, a long high facade of brown stone, with mullioned windows, romantic battlements, and a

31

high tower with a turret, referred to by the narrator in *The White Peacock* as 'the square tower of my old school'.

The final climb to the gates took Bert past the ornamental Arboretum with its miniature lake, flower-beds, winding paths and band-stand. The rest of the hillside was covered with newish houses and gardens, large or small, forming one of the town's best residential areas, where the very street-names – Waverley and Burns, Addison and Tennyson – were taken from literature.

Inside the school, Bert entered a new world, an all-male world in which there were no 'wenches' to soften the roughness of life, and no argument about Christian names. He was Lawrence, now, Lawrence, D. H. The masters were awe-inspiring figures in voluminous black gowns with square-topped tasselled mortarboards clapped on their clever heads. They were gentlemen with Oxford or Cambridge degrees. As well as letters after their names one or two had 'Rev.' in front. This must have pleased Mrs Lawrence, who had a high regard for parsons.

Not only were the masters themselves gentlemen, they were keenly concerned to turn out gentlemen from the school. The head, Dr Gow, was a humane and imaginative character, who gave his boys the same loyalty he expected from them. Once, when some shrubs had been damaged in the Arboretum, the police asked his help in tracing those responsible. 'I am not here to play detective for the police,' Gow retorted, 'but to defend the interests of my boys.' He said a quiet word to the school in assembly, and there was no more cause for complaint.

The best way to prevent trouble, he believed, was to keep the boys off the streets. The school playground was left open for them throughout the daylight hours. Those who lived close by could return and play when they had had their evening meal and done their preparation.

The staff followed his lead. He had gathered round

him some keen men who devoted their whole lives, sometimes more than forty years' service, to the school. Two such were the brothers, W. E. and W. T. Ryles, known as 'Jumbo' and 'Nipper' respectively, who were still there in the nineteen-twenties. 'Always remember,' Nipper admonished the new boys, 'if you wish to take off your jacket to play football in the playground, *a gentleman does not play games in his braces.*' He was saying that in 1920. It is a safe guess that Lawrence and his schoolfellows heard much the same instruction in 1898.

Apart from such opportunities to acquire more polished manners and speech, the school offered a good intellectual training by the standards of the time. True, only a minority of boys stayed until the end of their teens and went on to universities. More left at fifteen and entered business. That was as high as Mrs Lawrence's ambitions for Bert could fly – his scholarship was only for three years. But at the end of the nineteenth century many middle-class boys went no further. Meanwhile, they were given an education with a relatively modern bias. The High School was one of the first to give science an important place, and, while only a handful of pupils learned Greek, a great many (like Lawrence) studied German as well as French. As the great critic, F. R. Leavis, has said, Lawrence 'had a better education, one better calculated to develop his genius for its most fruitful use, than any other he could have got'.

It should have been wonderful. Yet somehow it was not. A certain obscurity hangs over those High School years. Whatever memories they left in Lawrence's mind, few traces are visible in his written work. He, who always drew so liberally on his own experience, transferring whole chunks of his life and building them almost without alteration into the fictional edifices of his novels, left this particular quarry practically unused.

In the same way, whereas friends and acquaintances have crowded forward from every other period, right back to his infancy – witnesses only too eager to recall anecdotes and impressions – biographers have never met with any rush of former schoolmasters and schoolfellows remembering Lawrence in classroom and playground.

He is a name on the register. His academic career is recorded in a few lines. But for that – and his carving his name on a fireplace – he might never have been.

What, if anything, went wrong?

Probably nothing much. Anything sensational would have been remembered by others, anything bitterly un-happy would have been remembered by Lawrence him-self, and it would have worked itself out in one of his books.

The answer to the enigma may well be simple and prosaic.

He was a 'train boy', and inevitably train boys could never quite belong. They were apt to arrive late and miss the opening assembly. When lessons ended, or even a few minutes earlier, they had to dash for the station. They could not linger in the playground or return there after tea. Out-of-school friendships had little chance to develop.

Further, Lawrence was a 'scholarship boy' among the sons of professional and business men. The gulf between the classes was wide. A scholarship had a smack of charity about it. The snobbery was not universal – not all boys showed it, and some only because their parents put it into their heads – but he was made aware of it. Once another boy invited him home to tea, discovered that his father was a miner, and then said that it was impossible for them to be friends. Lawrence, however, was sensitive and touchy, and probably did not make the most of what op-portunities he had. He merely recalled, in later years, that he had 'made a couple of bourgeois friendships, but they were odd fishes'.

After the first year he had the daily company of George Neville, another scholarship winner from the Beauvale School. Each morning the two Eastwood boys started out together in the blue peaked cap and the knickerbockers, or breeches fastening just below the knee over their long stockings, which were then uniform for the younger boys. Together they hurried each morning to Eastwood's nearest station, Newthorpe, and scrambled into the train. Together, at the other end of the journey, they hurried through the steep streets of the city.

They had a long day, stretching sometimes from seven in the morning until seven at night. It would have been a strain for any growing boy. Looking back, when ill-health dogged him in manhood, Lawrence blamed those journeys for undermining his constitution still further. The East Midland climate is not a kind one. The winters can be bleak, and Nottingham, sloping down into the broad valley of the Trent, is notorious for its fogs. They are nowhere worse than in the hollow through which the boys passed before climbing the last stiff incline to the school – the mist hangs dankly over the Arboretum pond. It did not help the hacking cough from which Lawrence suffered continually, even then.

His early delicacy, which had turned him away from strenuous games in childhood, now set a further barrier between him and his schoolfellows. This was the period when organised team sport was coming to its zenith in the British public schools. In such an atmosphere the boy who did not distinguish himself at games was of little account.

Lawrence could have made his mark if he had excelled intellectually, but he did not. He was a mediocre scholar. The competition was keen – there were clever boys head-ing for the universities – and the physical exhaustion of those long days put him at a disadvantage.

Oddly enough, he did best in mathematics. In 1900 he won two prizes in this subject, whereas in English he – the future writer – came thirteenth in a class of twenty-one. He was thirteenth also in German. In French he sank to nineteenth.

His feelings about school subjects can be guessed from a passage in *The Rainbow*, where he has probably transferred his own experience to the character, Ursula Brangwen, whom he sends to the Nottingham Girls' High School, a quite separate school standing at the other end of the same street.

'Something in mathematics, their cold absoluteness, fascinated her ... the very sight of the letters in Algebra,' he wrote, 'had a real lure for her.' But 'the close study of English literature' she found 'most tedious'. 'Only in odd streaks', as on one afternoon, reading *As You Like It*, 'did she get a poignant sense of acquisition and enrichment and enlarging from her studies.'

It was with much the same reactions that Lawrence plodded through those three years, anxious to please his mother and live up to the shining example of his brother Ernest. The nineteenth century drew to its close. The school hummed excitedly with news of victories and disasters far away in South Africa, where the might of the British Empire was finding it unexpectedly difficult to defeat the Boer settlers. Dr Gow started a cadet corps. They drilled, did rifle-practice, paraded to church, and endured long route marches of up to twenty-two miles. It was just another school activity in which Lawrence did not take part.

The twentieth century dawned. Lawrence was fifteen. He was in the Modern Sixth, struggling to hold his own with eighteen other boys, mostly older than himself. His

form-master was a cultured, eccentric and popular character named Sammy Corner, whose working life had been
devoted to the school under three headmasters. Another
pupil, about this period, has described him as 'an elderly
man who, in the winter-time, wore all day long two over-
coats under his tattered gown, a woollen scarf round his
neck and mittens on his hands, the whole crowned by a
mortar-board which always seemed to be the worse for
wear'. If Lawrence felt the cold half as much as his form-
master it is hardly surprising that his cough remained.
Men like Corner were the real-life prototypes of fictional
characters such as 'Mr Chips' – but that was not the kind
of fiction Lawrence was to write when he grew up. What
he thought of his teacher was never recorded for posterity.

Victoria died. The school shared in the wave of national
mourning. On the day of the funeral the cadets marched
down to the market place for the drum-head service,
watched by thousands of black-clad, moist-eyed townsfolk.
Once more, the miner's son from Eastwood was a little
detached from the majority, a little apart from the herd.
Already his circumstances and nature were pushing him,
by degrees, towards that isolation which characterised
him in later life.

It was in January that the Queen died. Her son,
Edward the Seventh, succeeded – himself already elderly,
but pleasure-loving and immoral, though the hypocrisy
of the age hushed up the scandal because royalty must be
respected. His reign was to open a new epoch. Everything
(people said) would be different now. The young hoped
life would be gayer and freer, no longer stuffy with the
conventions that had gathered during the sixty-three years
of the Victorian regime.

In May Lawrence began his last term at school. In July
his three-year scholarship would expire and he must look
for work. His family could no longer keep him. The fif-

teen pounds a year paid no more than his tuition fees and train fares. Even without avoidable extras like the cadet corps, it had been a financial sacrifice. And even if there had been all today's public provision, which allows the poorest boy or girl in Britain to go on to a university, there was little in Lawrence's work that would have encouraged him to seek a place. In that final term he finished fifteenth out of nineteen.

Another phase in his education, however, was about to begin. That was the summer when, on one of his afternoons off, he paid his first visit to Haggs Farm and met Jessie Chambers.

3   HAGGS FARM

Though the boy and girl met for the first time that afternoon in 1901, Jessie had noticed Lawrence years earlier at Sunday School, and the two families were acquainted. Most people knew Jessie's father. He delivered milk and was a familiar figure in Eastwood, driving his horse-drawn cart from door to door and ladling the milk from the big metal churns into the jugs held out by the housewives. Jessie's elder sister, May, as already mentioned, used to visit the Lawrences, and the two mothers had struck up a friendship at church. But it was several years before Mrs Lawrence took up the invitation to visit the Chambers' home, and only then after Mr Chambers had told Lawrence of a short cut by which he could bring his mother through the fields.

Haggs Farm is the Willey Farm depicted in *Sons and Lovers*. It was really little more than a smallholding which Mr Chambers rented. Some of his fields lay four miles away and were quite separate. To make a living he needed the milk business as well.

The house was long and low, with a gable window. Honeysuckle and virginia creeper rioted over the walls, and the cream-painted window-frames stood out cheerfully against the russet brick. There was a little front garden, with wooden palings, and then the porch. At the back there were fruit trees, cherry and plum and apple, and bushes with the gooseberries and currants forming.

To Lawrence, coming from the streets of Eastwood, it was like another world, idyllic and beautiful. The approach, by field and woodland, made it seem infinitely more remote than the actual three miles from home. In the thinly disguised account of that walk in *Sons and Lovers*, 'The lake was still blue ... the wood, heaped on the hill, green and still. "It's a wild road, mother," said Paul. "Just like Canada." '

Gradually, as he paid weekly visits on his school half-holiday, he came to love the people as well as the place.

He did not at first have much to do with Jessie, later the model for 'Miriam' in the novel, 'a girl in a dirty apron' with 'a dark rosy face, a bunch of short, black curls, very fine and free, and dark eyes; shy, questioning, a little resentful of strangers ...' Though Lawrence had made contact with her, the friendship took time to grow.

Her elder brothers, Alan and Hubert, were also cautious to begin with, wary lest this High School Sixth Former should give himself airs. It was with their father, the kindly Edmund Chambers, that Lawrence most quickly made friends.

Mr Chambers had not much education himself but he respected it. He loved reading. The local newspaper was serialising Thomas Hardy's novel, *Tess of the D'Urbervilles*, and every week he would read aloud to his wife the latest long instalment. They both loved the books of James

Barrie, then known chiefly as a young novelist. Mr Chambers liked to discuss with the minister whether the Bible was literally true. He himself gave talks to the Christian Endeavour class and would sit up until two o'clock in the morning to prepare his material.

Mr Chambers talked to the fifteen-year-old schoolboy as though he were an equal – not a common attitude in an era when age and experience were so venerated. The rest of the family listened in silence while their father debated with Lawrence whether, for instance, it was possible to store electricity.

Of all the seven Chambers children Jessie was the least likely to interrupt. Whereas May was studying to become a teacher, Jessie felt herself a kind of Cinderella, snatched from school before she was ready, so that she could help in the house and look after her baby brother, David. What could *she* know about electricity?

So passed the first months of their acquaintance. Lawrence left school and started work. His visits became rarer. The long working week of that period, with no half-holiday, left little time or energy for six-mile walks.

In applying for his first job he had his brother's guidance. Ernest came home from London on a visit, splendid in his City clothes, knowledgeable about the great world, an obvious success. But the pleasure of his coming home was marred for his mother : he brought a girl with him.

Gypsy Dennis (what a name, thought the Lawrences!) was dark, vivacious, sophisticated, 'la-di-da' as the saying goes, and probably no better than she should be. She was one of the dangerous new creatures who were beginning to infest the more modern offices. Some employers called such girls 'typewriters', confusing them with their machines.

Gypsy appears in *Sons and Lovers* as 'Louisa Lily Denys Western'. Lawrence was to use almost everyone he

41

met as a character in his novels. Though more than once this brought him legal trouble he never learned caution, and would recklessly scatter identifying clues, as in this case with the names 'Dennis' and 'Denys'.

The girl thought of little but dancing and parties. The atmosphere took on an extra strain, as Mrs Lawrence's lips pursed in disapproval. Ernest was her favourite son. She did not want him to get the wrong sort of wife, perhaps she did not want him to get a wife at all.

Ernest was not so besotted with his London friend that he could not spare time to help his young brother word a letter applying for a job. A vacancy was advertised in the *Nottingham Guardian* for a post at Haywood's, an old-established firm manufacturing elastic stockings and surgical appliances. That same day Lawrence took pen in hand. Ernest supplied the conventional commercial jargon and a respectful letter was concocted in the boy's best handwriting.

'Gentlemen, In reply to your ad. in today's *G.* for a Junior Clerk, I beg to place my services at your disposal...' Lawrence gave his age and school record. He offered to furnish 'the highest references as to character and ability, both from my late masters and the minister in this town.' He concluded: 'Should you favour me with the appointment I would always endeavour to merit the confidence you place in me. Trusting to receive your favourable reply, I beg to remain, gentlemen, Yours obediently, D. H. Lawrence.'

He got the job. His school French and German helped, for he had to deal with orders from abroad. He sat on a high stool, in the Dickensian fashion of those days, copying letters and making out invoices. From time to time he was sent on errands into the work-rooms where women and girls were making or packing the goods.

The warehouse stood in Castle Gate, a long narrow

42

street with some shabby but still elegant eighteenth-century mansions, running up from the centre of the town to the castle on its precipitous sandstone crag. The whole setting is vividly sketched in *Sons and Lovers*. Lawrence describes the 'gloomy and old-fashioned' street, its 'low dark shops and dark green house-doors with the brass knockers, and yellow-ochred doorsteps projecting on to the pavement', all in such contrast with the life and colour of the vast market-place, only a few minutes' walk away, 'where the horse trams trundled' and on the open stalls lay 'fruit blazing in the sun – apples and piles of reddish oranges, small greengage plums and bananas'. That market scene recurs in *The White Peacock*: for years, from schooldays onwards, it was part of his life.

The castle comes in, too. Once a royal fortress, it had been completely rebuilt as a duke's mansion in Charles the Second's reign, gutted by rioters in the early nineteenth century, and refurbished as a municipal art gallery during the great Victorian movement towards popular education and culture. Its gardens were popular then, as they are now. In *Sons and Lovers* Clara and Paul stroll up there during their midday break, lean on the parapet above the precipice, and gaze out over the landscape, while round them the pigeons flutter and coo. It was familiar ground for Lawrence himself.

In describing the long days inside the warehouse the novel is equally true to his own experience. Only in one significant respect did he alter the picture. In the novel he gives a good-humoured, almost affectionate account of the work-girls with their incessant banter. In reality, the teasing of these rough, outspoken young women caused him agonising embarrassment, for the curious thing is that Lawrence – whose later writings were to become notorious for the four-letter words previously impermissible in print – was himself delicate of speech and

43

repelled by dirty jokes. So far had his mother's dominating influence prevailed over the rest of his background.

A director of the firm remembered him long afterwards as 'very quiet and reserved'. His occasional errands to the work-rooms involved facing a crowd of lively young women, whom his mother would have called 'common', and who were eager to seize any momentary break in the tedium of their twelve-hour day. Once they seized Lawrence – literally – and tried to pull off his trousers. Horrified, he struggled free and fled.

It has lately been noticed that the firm's catalogue included, along with all the illustrations of artificial limbs, supports and appliances, some quite irrelevant decorations depicting Polar bears, African warriors, and a phoenix. Was it from this date, one wonders, that the legendary bird acquired its fascination for Lawrence? Years later, in his novel *The Rainbow*, the craftsman Brangwen models a phoenix in butter. Then, when Lawrence discussed with his friends the idea of founding a Utopian colony together, the phoenix was to be their symbol. Later still, when publishing his work through the Florentine bookseller, Orioli, he adopted the phoenix as his personal emblem – and at the end it was a phoenix that was set up, appropriately, over his grave. Did it all go back to Haywood's warehouse where he worked during those autumn weeks in 1901?

The first week in October brought Nottingham's annual Goose Fair, a carnival which for several days completely disrupted the ordinary business of the town. What had begun in the Middle Ages as one of the great trading fairs had developed by this date into the concourse of swings, merry-go-rounds, slides, sideshows and menagerie it remains today. But in 1901 the showmen were still allowed to take over the market-place itself and cram it with their stalls and amusements, blocking all traffic and

44

filling the town-centre with a constant blare and jig of metallic music which penetrated even to the warehouses of Castle Gate and beyond.

People travelled long distances to enjoy 'all the fun of the fair'. It was unthinkable that even Ernest in London should miss it. He came down – this time mercifully without Gypsy Dennis. He stayed a night or two at Eastwood, and then went to his elder brother, George, who was married and settled in Nottingham. Ernest looked unwell. His shipping firm, indeed, had offered him a free voyage to the Mediterranean, but he had declined. He caught the train back to London on the Sunday night after the fair. He looked like death, but was determined to go to work the next morning. By the middle of the week a telegram from his landlady brought Mrs Lawrence rushing to his bedside. He had pneumonia complicated with erysipelas. He died without recognizing her. Mr Lawrence, urgently brought up from the pit, joined his wife in London but was too shocked to be of much help. She, as always, was the manager. Tight-lipped and heart-broken, she made the necessary arrangements for her favourite child to be taken home to Eastwood for burial.

The effect on her youngest son was catastrophic.

Not only had Lawrence lost the brother he had been taught to admire as a model, but for the moment he seemed to have lost his mother's love. Instead of turning to him for consolation, she shut herself off, obsessed with her grief.

Within another month Lawrence too was dangerously ill with pneumonia. Possibly his illness was induced by his psychological state, his need to win back his mother's attention, though his working conditions provided physical explanation enough. He was at the warehouse normally until eight o'clock in the evening, though on Thursdays and Fridays he might get away at six. Then there was the train journey and the walk home. And every morning, except Sundays, he would be turning out again in the cold autumn dawn to reach his desk by eight.

It was several days before the Chambers family realised how ill he was. They had ceased to expect frequent visits and at that date the telephone, though invented, played no part in ordinary people's lives. It was left to Mr Chambers to pick up the bad news as he drove round with the milk. His wife was much upset and a gloom fell upon the entire family. Daily Mr Chambers brought home reports on the boy's progress. All the Lawrences' neighbours spoke of this new trouble that had fallen upon the household. It would be a miracle if Mrs Lawrence did not lose her boy within a few weeks of the elder one.

But Lawrence's illness jerked the mother out of her brooding and restored something of her old fighting spirit. She nursed him devotedly. He could no longer feel neglected. Soon he was past the crisis and beginning to gather strength. He sent messages to Haggs Farm by Mr Chambers, asking to be visited.

It was May, not Jessie, who responded. One foggy Sunday evening she knocked on the door with a bunch of snowdrops from the garden. Mrs Lawrence welcomed her.

'Why, child! This black night! Aye, he'll be pleased to see you. I tell him his heart's more at your house than ours.'

May followed her upstairs. In a tiny room, which seemed to her no more than a big box, she found Lawrence smiling from amid the tumbled bedclothes – flushed, sunken-cheeked, restless, but smiling and bright-eyed, with something of the old gaiety she remembered. He questioned her eagerly. What was happening at Haggs? Had they missed him? He asked after all the family, the white bull terrier Trip, Flower the horse, and the two

46

pigs he had himself rechristened Dido and Circe. His voice was shaky. It is possible that the illness had permanently affected his vocal chords. A rather high-pitched voice was one of his characteristics in later life. Those who had known him before noticed the change.

When he was fit to go out of doors, Mrs Lawrence let him sit in the patch of garden, well muffled in a blanket, to enjoy the sunshine. Then one day, as the weather became really spring-like, Mr Chambers put him into the milk-cart and drove him up the quiet lane which ended at the Haggs. Jessie saw him through the kitchen window as he came up the path in a dark overcoat, looking much taller and frailer than she remembered him. 'How white he is!' exclaimed her mother. 'How thin, poor lad!' He came into the kitchen, and they could tell how delighted he was to see them again.

There was no question of returning to the warehouse. A long convalescence lay before him. They pressed him to visit the farm whenever he liked.

'Come up through the Warren,' Mr Chambers told him. 'You want to get the smell of them pine trees into your lungs. Good for weak chests, aren't they?'

Lawrence took them at their word. Haggs Farm became his second home. His mother grumbled that he might as well pack up and move there. Looking back, years later, he declared that he had been happy only when he was up at the Haggs.

He had made himself useful. As strength returned, he lent a hand with jobs. He joined Mr Chambers and the boys at haymaking in the distant fields that were to provide the setting for his short story, 'Love Among the Haystacks'. Apart from the work he did, he helped by keeping every one else cheerful. Mr Chambers loved him like another son. 'Work goes like fun when Bert's there,' he said. 'It's no trouble at all to keep them going.'

In the house Mrs Chambers found him just as helpful. Used to chores at home, Lawrence would get a fire going in the parlour grate, carry water for the boiler, or set the table. 'I'd like to be next to Bert in Heaven,' Mrs Chambers said.

There was plenty of play too. Saturday tea-time was a red-letter occasion every week. Lawrence brought cards and taught them to play whist. He got them dancing, acting, dressing up, singing songs. As in the hayfields he was the life and soul of the party. He convulsed them with comic imitations. Little David Chambers, the baby of the family, remembered him as 'a figure in a fairytale'. Towards the end of Lawrence's life he wrote to David, 'Whatever I forget, I shall never forget the Haggs – I loved it so. I loved to come to you all, it was really a new life began in me there ... Whatever else I am, I am somewhere still the same Bert who rushed with such joy to the Haggs.'

Jessie remembered too, and especially the fun at Christmas, when other young friends crowded into the farmhouse with Lawrence, as always, master of ceremonies. 'Then towards midnight,' she wrote, 'to escort our friends through the Warren and over the dim field path, singing, with the stars flashing above the silent woods, was perhaps the most wonderful bit of all ... Life in those days was full to the brim, pressed down and running over.'

This idyllic phase was vital to Lawrence's development. His early writings are bathed in the radiance of those days, but the books do not convey the full picture. One could not learn from the books Lawrence's capacity for light-hearted foolery, for becoming the natural and popular leader of a group, for sparking off general happiness and sharing it. The angry, earnest Lawrence of the later years obscures the high-spirited boy who once filled the farm parlour with laughter.

There were quieter times, too. There was much reading and discussing of books and magazines. If sometimes, in his own stories, Lawrence's farming folk seem remarkably and improbably intellectual, it must be remembered that his own characters were based primarily on the Chambers family. David, it is worth noting, became a professor of economic history and a highly esteemed scholar.

In those first months, when Lawrence resumed his visits, Jessie felt sadly at a disadvantage. She saw no future for herself. It was an age when girls were beginning to assert themselves as intelligent, independent individuals. But the odds were still heavy against them, and Jessie had little hope of escaping from the Cinderella role.

She did not speak her thoughts to Lawrence, but he seemed to divine them. Once, as they stood by the stable door, he took a stub of chalk from his pocket and wrote two Latin words across the wood. *Nil desperandum*.

'What does it mean?' she asked, though she knew well enough.

'Never despair.' He smiled mysteriously, and went off, forestalling further discussion.

What now? Lawrence's mother had been a teacher, May Chambers was training to become one, George Neville was choosing the same career – what more natural than that Lawrence should turn his thoughts that way? Soon, with his support, Jessie also was allowed to escape from the kitchen and start training.

The system in those days was one of 'pupil teachers'. Lawrence went to the Albert Street school near his home. Each morning he had an hour's instruction from the headmaster, Mr Holderness. For the rest of the day he had to teach his own class of about forty boys, tough colliers' sons whose fathers worked beside his own. It was not easy to command their respect. He looked back on it afterwards as 'savage teaching'. His starting pay was five pounds a year.

Jessie, meanwhile, was teaching girls at the same school. Lawrence asked her to look out for him and smile. He was nervous and needed comfort. Sometimes she dispatched a child to his classroom to get the correct time. He would send back a scribbled note, signed 'D.H.L.'

They saw a good deal of each other outside school. At first she was shy about going to his home.

'I know why you won't come,' he accused her. 'It's because of Father.' She tried vainly to deny it. She had heard such exaggerated tales of his drinking and she dreaded the encounter. 'There's nothing to be afraid of,' Lawrence insisted. 'You'd never see him. He's hardly ever in.'

The Lawrences had just moved round the corner into Lynn Croft. Jessie called, and he rather proudly showed her their new home. After that, most Thursday evenings, she walked down from the farm to visit the local library – it was open for only two hours each week – and she would go out of her way to call for him, so that they could choose their books together. Jessie was conscious of a special atmosphere in the house, 'a tightness in the air, as if something unusual might happen at any minute'. It was somehow exciting, yet it made her feel a little sick.

Lawrence called the new house 'Bleak House' because it stood open to the winds and looked across the rooftops in the valley to green fields and woods beyond. He liked to watch the clouds sailing across the meadows.

His mother belonged to the Women's Co-operative Guild and used to organise outings, hiring a 'brake', an open horse-drawn vehicle big enough to hold a party, for a long drive into the Derbyshire hills. Jessie and May used to join these parties with Lawrence. At other times the young people would make up a group of their own, perhaps as many as a dozen, and go by train.

One expedition on Good Friday, 1903, became a landmark in Jessie's memory. They had tramped to see an outcrop of rock, the Hemlock Stone. They were straggling along. Jessie paused to study the bronze tips of maple in the hedge. Glancing back, she saw Lawrence crouched in the middle of the road, struggling with an umbrella. He looked so intent, so anguished, that she asked what was the matter. It had been his dead brother's umbrella, he explained. 'Mother will be wild if I take it home broken.' She did not let him see that she had noticed his distress, but, she recorded later, 'this was perhaps the beginning of our awareness of sympathy for one another.' Lawrence too remembered the incident. It appears in *Sons and Lovers*.

Often they walked in the woods near the farm. 'The gamekeepers must often have seen us, but we never saw them,' she recalled. In fact, Lawrence had one very angry encounter when he and other friends were caught peering inquisitively through the windows of the shooting-box reserved for the gentry in the heart of the woodlands. But, though gamekeepers figure prominently in *The White Peacock* and *Lady Chatterley's Lover*, they played little part in his own experience.

Lawrence delighted in Nature. It was he who would find the robin's nest in the old kettle, the lark's nest in the crusted mud of an old hoofprint, the brown-blotched olive eggs of the peewit amid the ploughed furrows. He seemed to know every wild flower. Once she challenged him.

'How do you know what it is?'

'I *do* know.'

'But how do you know? You may be wrong.'

'I know – *because* I know.' He was growing angry. 'How dare you ask me how I know?'

That response foreshadows his arrogance in later life. He knew *because* he knew. How dared people ask how?

When Lawrence wanted to take Jessie to the Goose Fair – a late-night adventure amid the bright lights and wickedness of the city – her mother refused permission.

Lawrence went with his other friends and sent Jessie a vivid description of the fun they had had, under the title 'The Diary of a Butterfly to a Moth'. Jessie showed it to Mrs Chambers, who was vexed. 'What does he mean? Who is the moth? Are *you* the moth?' Jessie enjoyed her mother's anger. It helped to make up for the disappointment she had suffered.

In 1903 a new system of training began. Lawrence and Jessie had to go three days a week to the centre established in a Methodist chapel at Ilkeston, a small town three miles away. There was quite a party of Eastwood friends, including George Neville, 'the Diddler', as Lawrence nicknamed him. They caught the morning train, but often walked back across the fields at the end of the day. They were a tightly-knit band, and, being often in hot revolt against the views of their elders, they called themselves 'the Pagans'.

Soon they were joined by another student, Louise Burrows, who lived at the village of Cossall. Louise introduced a new element into Lawrence's life. Her father was a craftsman who ran a woodcarving class. Through him, Lawrence learned much of the then-prevalent artistic ideas of Ruskin and William Morris. In his novel, *The Rainbow*, Louie's father is depicted as the idealistic carver, while Louie herself was the model for 'Ursula', the student-teacher who is a central figure. Here Lawrence uses his experience of these years, boldly transferring it to a character of the opposite sex, one of the most difficult imaginative feats for any novelist. Lawrence, however, was the right man to attempt it. He had an unusual gift for understanding the feminine point of view, which is why he has left us, in his stories, such a gallery of memorable women. Even so, he would not trust entirely to this flair, but – with a humility not usual in other matters – would show drafts of what he had written and ask some

53

woman (Jessie was the first) if he had got the feminine psychology right.

The years of training carried him almost up to his twenty-first birthday. He was in no hurry to grow up – loth, Jessie thought, 'to admit that boyhood was over'. He had even resisted the idea of shaving as long as he could. May Chambers teased him as Jessie would not have dared to. 'You're not decent,' May told him, 'going about with that hairy, untidy face.' So Lawrence conformed. First he was clean-shaven, then he wore the small moustache fashionable with Englishmen at the beginning of the century. The beard familiar to posterity was grown during an illness in 1915, and kept perhaps as the rebellious symbol beards were by then becoming.

Meanwhile, as a student, he won more distinction than he had as a boy. In the King's Scholarship examination held throughout England and Wales, he topped the list. After passing another examination, he could have entered the University College at Nottingham and worked full-time for a degree, but he could not put down the fees. He had to teach at Eastwood for another year, saving every penny he could, while his mother in her turn made sacrifices to get the money together.

She hoped, Lawrence wrote in later years, that 'her son, who was clever, might one day be a professor or a clergyman ... That would have been rising in the world – on the ladder. Flights of genius were nonsense – you had to be clever to rise in the world, step by step.' He himself recoiled from this view.

Walking home with Jessie, he said one day : 'When an individual has more of any quality than other people, I think it ought to be shared. Don't you?' She agreed, and he went on: 'When one has bigger mental gifts, for instance, I think they ought to be used to help other people. That must be what they're given us for, don't

54

you think so?' He hesitated, groping for words. 'Perhaps I shall be something some day, I mean a bit more than ordinary ...'

Another time, he told her: 'Every great man – every man who achieves anything, I mean – is founded in some woman. Why shouldn't *you* be the woman I am founded in?'

He had begun writing poems and a novel he called *Nethermere*, later *The White Peacock*. He showed Jessie the first scraps of the story at Whitsuntide in 1906. He could not mention his writing to his mother, she would have scoffed at it, he feared, as affectation. But Jessie thought it wonderful.

They were spending so much time together that Mrs Lawrence tackled him. There was gossip, people were asking if he and Jessie were courting. His mother said he was not being fair to Jessie. They ought to be engaged or else not go about together. He might be blocking the girl's chances elsewhere. Lawrence examined his own feelings and decided that he did not love Jessie in that way, at least now. Clumsily, in a painful conversation which she set down afterwards, he broke it to her.

'This ... this friendship between us ... is it keeping even? Is it getting out of balance, do you think?'

'I think it is keeping in balance. I don't know what you mean.'

'I was afraid ... I don't know, you might be getting to care too much for me.'

Her heart turned cold. 'I haven't thought about it,' she lied. 'But why are you saying this?'

He explained then what his mother had said, the night before.

'Ah,' she said quietly, 'I always thought your mother didn't like me.'

Then it was his turn to be less than frank. 'It isn't that. You mustn't think that. Mother has nothing against you ...'

She felt the world spinning round her. She tried to hide her tears. She 'saw the golden apple of life that had been lying at my finger tips recede irretrievably.' Aloud she said, 'We'll have nothing to do with one another.'

'No,' he said, 'we have so much in common, we can't give it all up.'

The friendship survived, but altered. He began his delayed course at the College. She might have gone, too, the following year, but when he saw what the course was like he advised Mr Chambers against sending her. 'Don't let her go,' he said, 'it isn't worth while. They grind them all through the same mill. They'll make her just like all the others.'

He had begun with hope and interest, but he had quickly been disillusioned. He was older than most of his fellow students and resented being treated as a 'school kid'. He disliked having his work returned by one tutor, Miss Becket, marked with the instruction, 'Give me a *proper* essay next time.' She told him that some of his phrases were fine but others were ludicrous. He was not 'entirely incapable of writing, but mixed up some sense with a great amount of absurdity.' If the first half of that comment reads oddly today, there is some justice in the second. The despised Miss Becket had laid her schoolmarm's finger on a weakness from which his work was never to be completely free.

At first he had taken the more difficult course of study that would have led him to a London degree. He gave it up, and worked for the teacher's certificate. It meant practice-teaching in one of the Nottingham schools, where he had to work under a man whose methods revolted him. This man's pupils produced splendid conventional

56

essays, but only, Lawrence complained, by the 'absolute ruin of their spontaneous expression'. His own idea of teaching English was far ahead of his time.

The College classes and lectures bored him. 'I am sick of work,' he complained, 'there is no end to it ... I am slogging Latin – how I suffer.' Even in the lecture-hall he sometimes shut his ears to the lecturer and wrote scraps of his novel. The subject he enjoyed most was music.

The one member of staff he respected was Professor Ernest Weekley, head of the Modern Languages department. 'He really *is* a gentleman,' Lawrence admitted. 'He leans back in his chair and points to the blackboard, too elegant to get on his feet. And he addresses us as "gentlemen". He's sarcastic, of course.' But at this stage his contact with the eminent scholar was only slight.

Though Jessie was not at College with him, Louie Burrows was, and gradually his friendship with her developed. Louie was tall, dark and attractive, with a more passionate nature than Jessie's – 'passionate as a gipsy,' Lawrence said later, 'but good, awfully good, churchy'. She and Jessie were friends. The Burrows family had moved to the Leicestershire village of Quorn, and when Louie visited her old friends she was invited to stay at Haggs Farm.

All three were interested in writing. Lawrence laid down the law. 'Like most girls you are wordy,' he admonished Louie. 'Do try to be terse ... Don't be didactic ...' It was excellent counsel, but reads ironically when set against some of his most famous work. 'You are brighter than Jessie,' he assured her, 'more reliable, but you are not so powerful.'

In 1907 the local paper offered prizes for short stories. There were three separate classes of story, but no competitor was to enter more than one. Lawrence wanted to try with an entry of each type, so he submitted one in his

57

own name and persuaded the girls to lend their names for the other two. The one which won a prize, in the class for 'enjoyable Christmas stories', was *A Prelude*, under the nom-de-plume of 'Rosalind'. It was the entry bearing Jessie's name and address, and the setting, very appropriately, was Haggs Farm.

Louie took happily to College work. It was her name, not his, that was starred in the list as 'Specially Distinguished'. He worked well only when his interest was roused. Then, said one of his more sympathetic tutors, 'Botany' Smith, he was not so much 'possessed' with an idea as 'obsessed'. Perhaps the staff were not always as imperceptive as he thought.

In his second year he took Philosophy and discussed it eagerly with Jessie and her brother Alan. He helped her with her French. They talked about books they were both reading, Meredith's *Love in the Valley*, Tolstoy's *Anna Karenina*, Renan's *Life of Jesus*. Lawrence had now drifted far from the religion of his childhood. He no longer wanted to sit silent in chapel, accepting every word of the sermon. He yearned to leap up and debate with the preacher.

'The chapel system of morality is all based upon *Thou shalt not*,' he complained to Jessie. 'We want one based upon *Thou shalt*.'

Sometimes he took her to the Theatre Royal, whose impressive pillared portico crowned the steep slope of Market Street between the shopping centre and the Gothic university college in a quieter street beyond. They saw *Hamlet*, *Macbeth*, the grand operas of Wagner, the gayer pieces of Gilbert and Sullivan. The greatest stage stars then toured the provincial cities. Lawrence went by himself to see the world-famous French actress, Sarah Bernhardt, in *La Dame aux Camélias*. The play shook Lawrence to the depths. He was terrified, he told Jessie, lest one day he too, like the character in Dumas' drama, should fall under a woman's domination.

They went to the art gallery and discussed the exhibitions. And always there were country walks, which Louie often came over to join. She and Jessie were in constant correspondence.

In 1908 Lawrence and Louie were both awarded their teacher's certificates, first class. The girl immediately got a job in Leicester. Lawrence, though he had collected half a dozen distinctions, found it much harder, partly because he stuck out defiantly for a living wage and would take nothing under ninety pounds a year. Louie had accepted seventy-five.

All through that summer he divided his time between writing innumerable applications and helping with the hay or other farm jobs. Jessie noticed how much of his old gaiety he had lost. He did not particularly want to teach, but he needed the money.

'The worst of teaching is,' he told Jessie, 'it takes so much out of you and gives you nothing in return. You never know what you've done ... Manual work is much more satisfying. You can *see* something for all your pains.' He knew that he was weak in classroom discipline. 'You are so just,' he wrote to her. 'I guess you never punish the wrong kid. As for me, I put up with them until I can stand them no longer, then I land the nearest, and as likely as not, he's innocent.'

His supervisor had given him a fair assessment. 'Well-read, scholarly, and refined,' ran his report, 'Mr Lawrence will make an excellent teacher if he gets into the right place.' After mentioning certain weaknesses the supervisor concluded: 'He could do work quite unusually good, especially if allowed a very free hand.'

Time passed, the hay was cut, September came, they started harvesting the oats, and still Lawrence was copy-

59

ing out with work-blistered fingers the testimonials he now knew by heart. 'I have used pounds of paper,' he wrote to '*Ma chère Louise*'. There was painful suspense at half-past eight each morning and seven in the evening, but the postman brought only polite rejections, 'We beg to inform you that your application was not successful.' After another week of it he was warning Louie, 'I shall soon mark myself as "unsaleable goods", and withdraw from the market.'

It was not until October 7, long after the school term had started, that he secured a post at Croydon, just south of London, at ninety-five pounds a year. He hastened to the farm to say goodbye.

Desperate though he was to get work, he now seemed to Jessie 'like a man under sentence of exile'. She saw him to the gate in the dusk. He looked back at the house in which he had known such happy times. '*La dernière fois*,' he murmured.

She burst into tears. Her own feeling for him had never wavered, and she could not help herself, though he had made it painfully clear that he did not find her sexually attractive. Now he was tender. He kissed her and stroked her wet cheek. 'I'm so sorry,' he kept repeating in a dead voice. She knew what he meant.

'Never mind,' she said, 'it doesn't matter.'

But it did, more than she could say.

After two days in Croydon Lawrence wrote a letter so depressed and emotional that it seemed to Jessie 'like a howl of terror'. But within a week or two another letter, this one to Louie, said that he was 'rapidly getting over' his 'loneliness and despair'. The school was an imposing new building, with plenty of open space, 'all very nice', though the headmaster was a 'weak-kneed windy fool', so that discipline was slack and teaching a struggle. Like many people from the more northerly parts of England, Lawrence did not at first take to the southerners among whom he had come to live. They were 'glib, but not frank; polite, but not warm.'

Luckily he was lodging (in 'excellent digs') with a North Country couple, an education official married to a former schoolmistress, who mothered Lawrence. There was a little girl of five, Winnie, and a baby. Lawrence took to the children and they to him. Soon he was putting them to bed, supervising Winnie's prayers, and baby-sitting when Mr and Mrs Jones wanted to go out in the evenings.

Though he criticised the southern people, he was soon enthusiastic about the Surrey countryside. He wrote to Louie of the rounded valleys, the 'gorgeous foliage', the steep hills 'whose scarps are blazing with autumn'. And there were other local compensations – Croydon had a splendid public library. His letters to Jessie were full of recommendations to read this book or that. He was revelling in the banquet of literature now freely spread before him. Galsworthy, Conrad, Arnold Bennett, Turgenev, Verlaine, Baudelaire, Nietzsche, Pushkin, Dostoevsky, Maeterlinck, Cervantes, Euripides – his range was enormous, touching almost every country and period. As with everything in his life, his likes and dislikes were violent and personal.

To Louie his letters were more concerned with the tribulations of teaching. She was deeply unhappy in her Leicester post. He tried to comfort her, confessing, 'I have some days of despair myself.' That was true. Once he burst out to a Croydon colleague that he would rather work on a farm. 'I know a farmer at Eastwood who would take me on tomorrow.' Such moods passed. He was a success at teaching. So was Louie. After that one miserable term she moved to a village near her home, becoming 'headmistress' of the thirty children in the little school.

Lawrence was specially concerned with Art and Nature Study. He was ahead of his time in using free methods that did not stifle the spontaneous feelings of the pupils. And he was lucky to have superiors and colleagues who were tolerant of his unorthodox approach. The headmaster was by no means the 'fool' Lawrence had first thought him. Once he conferred with an inspector about the art work produced in Lawrence's classes. The two men sensibly agreed that, not being artists themselves, they were not competent to criticise. 'We had better be careful with this man,' said the inspector. So, unknown to Lawrence, some of the boys' pictures were sent off to experts at the Art Department at Kensington. The inspector brought them back to the headmaster on his next visit. 'Good thing we took the course we did,' he said. 'The Department highly approves.'

When it came to producing the school play, Lawrence was struck by the talent of the boys from a home for actors' children close by. 'These actor boys,' he told the headmaster, 'know more about this sort of thing. Let them run this show as they think fit.' He contented himself with painting the scenery.

He was equally tolerant in the school library. 'Let them read any rubbish they like,' he pleaded, 'as long as they read at all. They'll very soon discard the bad.'

He could afford to give his pupils freedom because he never lost ultimate control. 'I have tamed my wild beasts,' he wrote to Louie in his second term, 'I have conquered my turbulent subjects, and can teach in ease—'

The same confidence came out in a poem he wrote, 'The Best of School', evoking the calm of his classroom on a summer morning:

> The blinds are drawn because of the sun,
> And the boys and the room in a colourless gloom
> Of underwater float ...
> ... and I,
> As I sit on the shores of the class, alone,
> Watch the boys in their summer blouses
> As they write, their round heads busily bowed.

From time to time a head is raised to look at him, and he feels

> ... the stream of awakening ripple and pass
> From me to the boys ...

He knows he has communicated, roused their interest,

given them what they were looking for. The poem ends:
... their thrills are mine.

Outside school, life was less calm. He wrote to Louie, sending her a volume of Ibsen's plays for her twenty-first birthday, and spoke of 'a host of difficulties'. He was 'short of money and worse than that'. He did not specify the second shortage, but it could have been guessed. He was twenty-three himself, unmarried and with no relief for the mounting pressure of his sexual instincts. 'Do you think J., you and I could make a happy triangle?' he asked. 'Somebody has a bad time when we three meet. Do you not feel it?'

Neither girl joined the young people's holiday party that Mrs Lawrence arranged, that summer, on the Isle of Wight. George Neville and several of the old Eastwood group were there, but Louie had already fixed a visit to the Lake District and Jessie probably kept away because of Mrs Lawrence's dislike for her. Mrs Lawrence would always stand between them. Her disapproval of Jessie, her possessive feelings for her son, and the son's abnormal devotion to his mother, made a formidable barrier. Lawrence enjoyed the holiday with his other friends. They hiked and bathed, watched the famous Cowes Regatta and a naval review in honour of the Russian Tsar, and sailed round the island in a steamer. His impressions later went into his second novel, *The Trespasser*.

That autumn he developed a new friendship with a girl teaching at another Croydon school. Helen Corke was an attractive *petite* young woman with a fiery temperament, advanced views, and a love of literature and country walking like his own. She was then just recovering from a severe emotional crisis. She had been involved in a passionate affair with her violin-teacher, a married man. They had gone away together – also, by coincidence, to the Isle of Wight. The affair had ended tragically, for the musician had returned home and committed suicide.

Lawrence incorporated Helen's story into *The Trespasser*, and for once the compliment was repaid: Helen eventually wrote and published a novel, *Neutral Ground*, in which Lawrence was depicted. The friendship was valuable to both of them. In Helen, Lawrence found some one with whom, like Jessie, he could discuss his writing. But despite her advanced views and an unchaperoned visit to the seaside, when their landlady showed them to rooms at 'opposite ends of a corridor' but then 'left the house', there is no evidence that they ever became lovers.

Meanwhile Jessie and Louie, though far away, were emphatically not out of mind. Jessie, of course, he saw at frequent intervals, for he often went home at week-ends as well as for the holidays. Meetings with Louie in Leicestershire were not quite so easy to arrange, but he made up for that by correspondence. From the period he spent at Croydon, rather more than three years, 126 letters and postcards to Louie survive, and have been published since her death.

Both girls, on separate occasions, came to visit him and see the sights of London. Jessie was given a room at his lodgings. It was late when they got there, for they had been to a theatre in the West End. Mr and Mrs Jones had gone to bed. Lawrence warmed up some macaroni in a saucepan for their supper, and then, clearing away the dishes, covered the table with pages of manuscript, poems she had never seen and a play, *A Collier's Friday Night*. It was after midnight and the exhausted girl had left home at six to catch the train. Unable to concentrate, she asked if she could take the manuscripts home to read properly. He agreed, and gathered them together.

'Now we'll talk.' He hesitated. 'But perhaps you want

65

to go to bed?' he said discouragingly. 'Can you give me another hour?'

She could not refuse him. They stayed talking until two o'clock. He spoke of his longing to get married. 'But I've no money,' he lamented. 'I shan't be able to marry for ever so long. I think I shall ask some girl if she will give me ... that ... without marriage. Do you think any girl would?'

Jessie was tired and utterly miserable, knowing the hopelessness of her own love for him. She had to bend her head so that he could not see her tears.

'I don't know,' she said. 'The kind of girl who would, I think you wouldn't like.'

He persisted. 'Would *you* think it wrong?'

'No, I wouldn't think it wrong. But all the girls I know would.'

It was 1909, the year in which H. G. Wells had dared to depict, in *Ann Veronica*, a heroine who believed in votes for women, sex-equality, and love if necessary outside the marriage-tie. The book had shocked many people, been denounced in the press, and banned by the libraries. It had also sold extremely well.

Lawrence repeated his question. 'But *you* wouldn't?' It could scarcely have been meant as a personal appeal. He had just told her of a Croydon teacher he might be getting engaged to – he had arranged to introduce the two girls to each other in the morning. The teacher was not Helen Corke but a tall red-headed girl named Agnes Holt.

'Not *wrong*,' said Jessie. 'But it would be very difficult.'

He was silent. Then, his mind obviously running on Agnes Holt, he said: 'Well, I think I shall ask *her*. Do you think she would?'

Not yet having met her, Jessie could only say: 'It depends on how much she is in love with you.' She went on:

'Look, Bert, it's two o'clock. I really am tired now.'

'Very well, I'll let you go,' he conceded reluctantly with the thoughtlessness of the young male obsessed with his own desires.

There is no evidence that Agnes Holt ever allowed him to make love to her. Soon afterwards Lawrence told Jessie that the idea of marrying Agnes had been a mistake, that she had left Croydon and passed out of his life. At this stage he seems to have had at least seven close emotional friendships. There were two other women, never positively identified, in Croydon – a 'Mrs Davidson' and a 'Jane'. There was Helen Corke. At Eastwood there was the chemist's young wife, Mrs Dax, well known as an extreme propagandist for Socialism, votes for women, and other causes. She gave Lawrence the model for 'Clara Dawes' in *Sons and Lovers*. She gave him also the physical love he was so frenziedly seeking. She was probably the only one of the seven who did.

That Christmas Lawrence and Jessie talked at leisure. His feelings for her were violent but confused. At times he had said, 'I can't *make* myself love you, can I?' and she had answered, 'Why don't you leave me alone?' He could not. 'You are necessary to me,' he insisted. On another occasion he said, 'Some part of me will *always* want you.' He called her, 'the anvil on which I have hammered myself out.' She accepted the role of anvil, but it was a painful one. According to her account, published a quarter of a century later, they now entered into a secret engagement, telling nobody. People 'would make such a fuss and ask so many questions.' Lawrence told her that their years of friendship had been a preparation for this, but he had only just realised that it was she whom he had loved all along. She was aware of a forced note in his voice, as though he were trying to convince himself, but her love swayed her to believe in his sincerity.

67

It was to her that he showed his writings, and it was Jessie who took the decisive step of copying some from the rough scraps of paper on which he had jotted them, and submitting them to the *English Review*, a handsomely-produced new literary magazine. The editor, Ford Madox Hueffer, accepted them at once and asked Lawrence to call on him. A month or two later, on that turbulent weekend when Jessie stayed in Croydon, the two young people were asked to Sunday lunch at the Kensington home of Violet Hunt, a novelist closely associated with Hueffer and his magazine. There was a young American poet among the guests, who sat next to Jessie and was the life of the party. He was the same age as Lawrence and also destined for fame – he was Ezra Pound. Hueffer, by this date, had been telling many influential literary people of the new writer from Nottinghamshire he had discovered. That Sunday, however, Violet Hunt took care to give Jessie the credit that was her due. 'But you discovered him,' she said.

Lawrence's poems began to appear prominently in the *English Review*, followed by his short story, 'Goose Fair'. Hueffer took him to literary parties. He began to meet famous writers like Wells and W. B. Yeats, painters, and actresses. He was launched. But it meant little in terms of money. Each morning he faced his class again in Croydon.

In his first year there he had completed the novel he had been writing and rewriting since before his entry to College. Hueffer and Violet Hunt said they would help him to find a publisher. In January 1910 Lawrence was able to tell Louie that the book was 'practically accepted'. He had been up to see William Heinemann, the famous publisher, who had read him the readers' reports, 'mostly good'. He had to alter a few passages. Some months later, with the book already in production, he told her he had been asked to choose another title. So *Nethermere* became *The White Peacock*.

It is easy to pick holes in this novel. It is narrated in the first person by a vague, anaemic character named Cyril, apparently without regular occupation though he has artistic leanings and often (like the author) helps with the work on the farm which figures so prominently in the story. A serious flaw is his tendency to describe intimate scenes between the other characters, scenes at which he could hardly have been present, or it would have been extremely odd if he had. There are too many adjectives, there are archaic literary words such as 'perchance'. For all his rewriting, Lawrence can be caught out in careless slips – on the very first page, the repetition of 'lazy' within four lines scarcely looks like deliberate art. The beautiful descriptions are tiresomely full of what Ruskin called 'the pathetic fallacy', the attribution of human feelings to objects in Nature. Lawrence's daffodils 'nod to one another in gossip', the water of the mere is 'eager', the young morning wind 'moans at its captivity'. Yet, in his case, it could be argued that he was not following an outworn literary fashion, but expressing a genuine emotion within himself. 'He seemed to know, by personal experience,' wrote his friend, Aldous Huxley, many years later, 'what it was like to be a tree or a daisy or a breaking wave or even the mysterious moon itself.' It was all part of the intensity with which he felt the wholeness of Life.

With all Lawrence's writing – as with his personality – it is not very profitable to pick holes. The flaws must be faced honestly. But then, if one is to appreciate Lawrence, it is better to turn to his strong points. Taken by itself as a novel, *The White Peacock* is a lyrical evocation of the English countryside in the final era of pre-scientific, pre-mechanised farming at the beginning of the twentieth century.

For the understanding of Lawrence, the book has another importance. It contains so much of his own life up to that date. The countryside is there, and the mining area, the 'tapering chimneys marked in black against the swim of sunset', the colliers 'squatting on their heels against the wall'. Nottingham is there, castle and market place and theatre, and the pleasure-steamers puffing down the Trent. Cyril in Norwood (like Lawrence in Croydon a few miles away) suffers acutely 'the sickness of exile', though Emily tells him enviously: 'At home you cannot live your own life. You have to struggle to keep even a little apart for yourself. It is so hard to stand aloof from our mothers ...' Was the author striving to say something here to his own mother that he could not say to her face?

Whatever his motive, he was longing for the day when he could place the first printed copy in her hands.

The tormenting relationship with Jessie continued. Her family had moved to another farm on the northern fringe of Nottingham. He arranged to spend some days there in August, but that visit did not take place. They had met previously at Eastwood. There had already been friction over Helen Corke. Lawrence had just finished *The Trespasser*, a story in which Jessie had no part. 'For this I need Helen,' Lawrence explained. 'I must *always* return to you, only you must always leave me free.' Jessie was not going to share him. She wanted 'complete union or a complete break'. 'Then I am afraid it must be nothing,' he said. That was the end of their secret understanding. They agreed to give up writing letters, but they could not keep to that. The bond between them was too strong.

That same August Mrs Lawrence was taken ill while visiting her sister in Leicester. She was stranded there for some time, and Louie paid her some friendly visits. It was soon clear that she had cancer, a disease most people shrank from even naming in those days, since modern treatments were as yet undiscovered and the mere word rang like a death-sentence. So it proved with Mrs Lawrence. She was taken home to Eastwood, but all through that autumn she was dying, slowly and painfully, growing ever weaker.

Lawrence came up from Croydon every other weekend. He was strained and desperate, watching his mother die. He had no illusions. She could scarcely last into the new year when his novel would be published – he could not wish her to, he loved her too passionately to want her sufferings prolonged, he only wanted her now to be at rest.

He asked Heinemann's to hasten the production of his book so that at least he could show her an advance copy, while she was still conscious and able to understand. At last he got the book. It looked, he thought, 'very nice', but he had no heart to open it, except to write a tiny inscription inside. He put the book into his mother's hands. She glanced at it but without any animation. Lawrence's sister prompted her: 'It's yours, my dear.' 'Is it?' She closed her eyes wearily. Later she revived enough to ask: 'What does it say?' The inscription was read to her. She made no comment and did not refer to the book again. It had all come too late.

Some weeks before that, Lawrence had found her still well enough to discuss another matter. He was looking ahead to the emptiness that awaited him when his mother was gone. More than ever he needed to marry. His feeling for Louie Burrows had surged up – he could imagine a warm, happy life with her. She would never make the demands on him that Jessie, in her intensity, would have done. She would never, as he explained to a friend, 'demand to drink me up and have me'. It was his old horror of being dominated by a woman.

Cautiously he sounded his mother. 'Would it be all right for me to marry Louie – later?'

'No,' said Mrs Lawrence promptly. It was her reflex action to the idea that her son should marry any one. But, after a pause, she must have reflected that Louie was at least far preferable to Jessie, whom she hated – 'she would have risen from the grave,' said Lawrence, 'to prevent my marrying *her*.' Grudgingly Mrs Lawrence revised her verdict. 'Well,' she said, 'if you think you'd be happy with her – yes.'

Lawrence proposed to Louie in the train from Leicester to her village. It was an unromantic setting, with five local women crowding the compartment and able to eavesdrop on their conversation.

Louie asked, 'What do you think you'll do, Bert – after Christmas?'

'I don't know,' he said. Then he looked at her and went on, 'I should like to get married. Should *you*?'

She flushed scarlet and pretended to be looking out of the window. 'What?' she said.

'Like to marry me?'

She turned her face then, and it was radiant. 'Later,' she said.

The train was slowing down for her station. 'We're at Quorn!' he said in dismay.

She leant forward and laid her hand on his. 'I'll go on to Loughborough. I can come back by the 8.10.'

The other women got out at Quorn. The two lovers were alone as the train ran on through the December dark.

Six days later Mrs Lawrence died. He was with her at the end, an end he had come to long for. It is all in *Sons and Lovers*, the anguish of the too-devoted son watching his mother's drawn-out agony. Afterwards, in outlining the theme of that novel to Edward Garnett, he also described the relationship which had bedevilled his own efforts to find satisfactory love from a girl of his own age. A woman's two sons, when they come to manhood, 'can't love, because their mother is the strongest power in their lives, and holds them,' he explained. In the case of the younger son, Paul Morel – clearly himself, the girl 'fights for his soul – fights his mother.' The battle rages with the son as object, but the mother 'proves stronger, because of the tie of blood', and when she begins to die the son 'casts off' the girl he has loved. This, in real life, was Jessie. Lawrence told himself, when his mother was dead, that there would be no similar problem with Louie.

On the day before the funeral he went for a walk with Jessie along the lanes they had often followed happily as students. She reproached him for becoming engaged to Louie. She thought he was merely running away from reality. She said, 'You oughtn't to have involved Louie in the tangle of our relationships.'

His cold reply took her breath away. 'With "should" and "ought" I have nothing to do.'

They paused beside the railway leading to the mines. He tried to explain. In a choking voice he said, 'You know – I've always loved Mother.'

'I know you have.'

'I don't mean that. I've loved her – like a lover. That's why I could never love you.'

6 THE ENGAGEMENT

'I am so tired,' Lawrence wrote to Louie. The funeral was just over, the mourners departed. Most of the arrangements had fallen on his shoulders, and now he had to catch the train and finish the last week of term at Croydon. Though his mother's death had been expected, it had been (he wrote long afterwards) 'the great crash', marking the end of his youth.

Life went on. There was the end-of-term party at school, a visit to the dentist, a consultation with a schools inspector about his chances of getting a job in the country ... Christmas shopping – amid all the family grief, the little nephews and nieces must have presents and so must the children at his lodgings ... and Christmas itself must be spent somewhere. Rather reluctantly, he was going to the seaside with his sister, Ada, who badly needed a change after the ordeal of the past few months.

Lawrence begged Louie to join them near Brighton : she countered with an invitation to her home. He said he was 'too shy' to make a long visit, but it was arranged that he should go up to Leicestershire for the New Year week-end.

Meanwhile, in those last three weeks of 1910, he wrote to her eleven times. 'I want you so much I daren't say anything ...' 'If I could put my arms round you ...' 'A kiss – good God – not one.' He addressed her as 'My dear Lou', 'Carissima', 'Geliebte' and 'Dear Little Ousel', but however hungrily passionate his closing phrases they were always followed by the signature 'D. H. Lawrence' or 'DHL'.

There was much to discuss. He had to satisfy Louie's doubts about all those other girls. The affair with Jessie, he explained, he had allowed to run on 'unawares'. She remained his 'very dear friend', but that was all. He confessed that he had been 'a fool' about 'the other three', they had only liked and flattered him. One (this was Agnes Holt) was 'a jolly nice girl', teaching in Yorkshire and already engaged to someone else. 'One is a little bitch, and I hate her,' he went on viciously, perhaps referring ungratefully to Mrs Dax, for he added that 'she plucked me, like Potiphar's wife'. The third of the un-named women, he protested, 'is nothing'.

Satisfied on these matters, and accepting his assurance, 'I shall be true and try to make you happy', Louie still had to face the prospect of a long engagement. Lawrence had no money. They agreed that they could not marry until he had increased his salary and saved at least a hundred pounds. His father was working very little now, his earning days would soon be over, and Lawrence would have to help. The predicament of the young lovers can be imagined only if one remembers the conditions of England in 1911. It would be another five years before the old miner qualified, at seventy, for one of the tiny Old Age Pensions that had just been introduced. Louie herself

75

would have to give up teaching if she married Lawrence – not until World War Two did married women teachers win the right to continue at work. There were no child allowances, no family planning clinics, no national health service ... However ardent the lover, if he was also a responsible young man, he dared not take a wife until he was able, without help from any one, to support her and the children who would most probably follow.

As for conducting a secret love-affair, while Louie kept on her own job, even if the girl had been willing to do anything so contrary to her nature, such subterfuge too often ended in disaster. Towards the end of that same year their old friend Neville had to marry in haste and secrecy, two months before the birth of a child – after which he had to leave the district in disgrace, take a poor temporary job and live by himself, while his wife and baby lived with her family fifty miles away. Neither Louie nor Lawrence wanted anything but respectable marriage. 'We can have infinite patience if need be,' he assured her.

It was not 'rash', he said when she criticised his applying for a post in Cornwall, he had merely shown 'promptitude in action'. As Louie did not want to live in that distant region he tore up his application – but when he saw a similar post advertised there he ignored her wishes and wrote off for it. He did not get the job.

If he could not secure promotion as a teacher, there was still his writing – though he tried not to delude himself, or her, with exaggerated hopes of what his books would earn. *The White Peacock* came out that January. Heinemann's paid him an advance of fifty pounds, equal to half a year's salary at his Croydon school. Lawrence's father looked at him as if he had got the money by false pretences. 'Fifty pound?' he echoed. 'An' tha's niver done a day's work in thy life!'

Work to him meant wielding a pick at the coal-face. His son's four years of writing and revision did not count.

For a week or two Lawrence waited for the press reaction. It was slow. An unknown first novel was seldom reviewed at once. Then, one by one, the clippings trickled in. The *Times* was hurtful: Lawrence confessed to Louie that he felt 'cut down like a poppy'. Another critic mentioned 'flashes of real genius' – but that was in the *English Review*, where favour might be expected. In total, the critical reception showed a fair balance between good and bad. The main objection was to the absence of 'a well-knit plot', 'aimlessness' and 'formlessness'. These were reasonable criticisms by the standards against which novels were measured at the time. But Lawrence was never interested in plots or in form. The value of his work would always lie in the 'force and power' which one reviewer recognized. For all Lawrence's incessant rewriting of his books – a habit he continued throughout his career – the effect was seldom what other authors aimed at, an improvement in construction and a tautening of the prose. What concerned him was the emphatic communication of what he had to say. Like an ill-advised orator, jumping to his feet for the second time, he was quite likely in his vehemence to go on too long and to repeat himself.

Some of the reviewers were oddly mistaken. More than one thought that *The White Peacock* had been written by a woman. The characters, it was objected, 'were spun in the author's brain'. This was particularly ironical. Lawrence had begun his life-long practice of drawing his characters from his own acquaintance. To say this is not to detract from his genius. He was much more than a human camera, aiming an impersonal lens. His eye for external detail was as shrewdly selective as it was keen, but he went far beyond the superficial features that present themselves to the casual observer. Lawrence's wonderful gift – as many who knew him have emphasised – was a deeper capacity for observation and understanding, that penetrated to the very core of the individual. His very hatred of conventional attitudes and artificial poses made him impatient of outer layers. As the critic, G. S. Fraser, has put it, he looked for 'the deep drives'. Finding them, identifying them, incarnating them in the person depicted, he gave each character a peculiarly dynamic quality.

That quality – though he could hardly have foreseen the result – has since contributed immensely to the success of Lawrence's fiction when filmed or dramatised in other media in later days. Actors and actresses love, above all things, a strong part they 'can get their teeth into'. Lawrence has provided such parts. Also, because his ear was as unerring as his eye, he has provided the other essential that actors demand – speakable dialogue. Open any novel of Lawrence's from *The White Peacock* to *Lady Chatterley's Lover* and this ingredient is there from first to last: crisp dialogue (surprisingly terse and economical compared with the rest of the text) and every line so authentically 'in character' that the speaker's identity scarcely needs to be indicated. Lawrence's potential as a playwright was never recognised while he lived – his attempts to write for the theatre met with little success and it was not until many years after his death that such plays as *The Widowing of Mrs Holroyd* and *A Collier's Friday Night* awakened people to this further aspect of his bewildering versatility. But his gift for writing dialogue, dialogue which both heightens the emotional intensity of an episode and simultaneously conveys the character of each speaker, is evident in the novels and short stories.

The habit of drawing those characters from the real life around him was inseparable from his method of work and contributed immensely to the fineness of that work, but it carried with it a practical disadvantage, indeed a danger. Within a month of *The White Peacock*'s publication he was threatened with legal action: 'Alice Gall' in the novel was recognisably one of the old Eastwood group, Alice Hall – Lawrence could not have taken much less trouble to disguise the connection – and Alice was now married. If her angry husband brought a libel action, it would probably mean the withdrawal of the book and the blighting of Lawrence's literary career at the very start, not to mention legal costs that might bankrupt him. Fortunately a good angel intervened. Willie Hopkin, an older friend of Lawrence's who for the rest of his long life remained his loyal champion, went as a peace-maker. Alice's husband belonged to the Society of Friends. Was it consistent with his beliefs that he should hound Lawrence through a court of law? Hopkin persuaded him. Lawrence was able to continue his career as a novelist.

The White Peacock sold well enough to require reprinting in March. It had come out also in the United States. But for the time being there was no more money. Heinemann's made up their royalty statements only once a year. Nor were there, in those days, the swift offers for film rights, paperback rights and other subsidiaries which now occasionally – but very occasionally – bring wealth to a new author overnight.

Lawrence was not in the best condition to make the most of what modest success he had had. His mother's death had left lingering effects upon him. His vitality was low – and much of it was needed to control his boys in the Croydon classroom. Even if publishers and editors had been pestering him with offers of well-paid work, he could hardly have responded. They were not. He could only go on, as well as he could, with the rewriting of his Isle of Wight novel. There was a snag even about that.

He had a pact with Helen Corke that, since he had used a situation in her private life, he would not publish for five years.

Already in 1910 he had begun a third novel, *Paul Morel*, which was to become *Sons and Lovers*, and this was passing through the usual long processes of rewriting. He did not at first tell Jessie about it, though it was woven from the early experiences in which she had played such an important part. Louie was apt to be jealous if she heard that letters were still passing between them. 'How strange of you to be angry with J. for writing,' Lawrence rebuked her. 'It certainly wasn't an amatory epistle.' Jessie for her part felt a natural resentment when she heard that Louie was flaunting her copy of *The White Peacock* as the work of the clever young man she was going to marry. Jessie had had so much to do with the creation of that book. 'I its creator, you its nurse,' Lawrence had acknowledged. Now she learned of the new work in progress from Helen Corke. Lawrence had introduced the two girls and, as Jessie did not regard Helen as a rival for his love, they had become good friends. In 1911 they spent much of their school holidays together, Helen visiting the Chambers farm outside Nottingham, Jessie staying with the Corke family in Croydon.

It was in the autumn of that year that Lawrence sent Jessie a big sheaf of manuscript and asked for her opinion. He had written about two-thirds of *Paul Morel* and seemed to be stuck. Reading it, she saw how autobiographical it was, but it lacked life. It was the writing of a tired man, forcing himself along. Comparing it with the reality, as she vividly remembered it herself, she was dismayed and disappointed. In places the story was sentimental, story-bookish. Important elements had been left out, such as the relationship with his dead brother Ernest.

She felt that Lawrence was missing the chance to write

a magnificent story. For him it was a mistake to depart from his own experience and to substitute fictitious situations. She felt also that if, in rewriting, he could relive the personal experience with complete integrity, he might get that strange obsession with his mother out of his system. Not only might a good book come out of it but, more important, 'a liberated Lawrence'. He might 'walk into freedom, and cast off the trammelling past like an old skin'. The thought must have occurred to her that this liberation might also extend to his engagement. Jessie was not alone in thinking that Lawrence had 'got the wrong girl'. His brother had told Lawrence so in those very words. And to Jessie herself George had scoffed at the notion that the marriage to Louie would ever take place. 'Married?' he exclaimed. 'I don't *think*, I *know* they'll never get married. Never in this world!'

Any such thoughts, or hopes, Jessie kept to herself. In returning the manuscript she confined herself to literary criticism. She urged him to write the whole story again and keep it true to life. He took her advice. More than that, he asked her to jot down her own recollections of their early days together, which he admitted were more vivid than his own.

Meanwhile, whether or not George Lawrence was justified in his pessimistic prophecies, it is clear from the letters his younger brother poured out to Louie all through that year that the separation was proving a strain.

Meetings were few and precious. Jessie came down to Croydon in March and in the Easter holidays Lawrence visited her in the Midlands, though much of that time had to be spent with his family, who had moved following his mother's death. In June all the schools had a special holiday for the coronation of King George V. Lawrence spent it with his family in Eastwood and Nottingham, probably because he was counting on a visit from Louie in Croydon. This did not take place, but they had a whole fortnight to look forward to in August, when the plan was for a large group of young friends, including Ada Lawrence and George Neville, to take a cottage on the Welsh coast.

Unfortunately, people dropped out. The party dwindled to Ada and themselves. Louie's mother began to have doubts. Lawrence wrote vehemently to Louie, dropping into French as he was apt to do in confidential passages. 'No matter what is said,' he insisted, 'we are going to Prestatyn on the 29th, you, I and Ada ... Tell your mother our plans bluntly, and allow no questions. My god – are we children?' The holiday took place without trouble, and soon afterwards he went to stay with Louie and her family at Quorn.

Even the simplest holiday, the cheapest railway ticket – without which he could not see Louie at all – put a strain upon his finances. His boots were down-at-heel, his shirts patched. In July, when Hueffer had invited him to a famous London club, he had been forced to decline because he had no presentable suit. It was hard when Louie, yearning for marriage and a home, nagged him for not saving every penny that his writing earned.

It was not, at the moment, earning him much. Hueffer, who had begun by promoting him so enthusiastically, was now up to his neck in troubles of his own, a divorce which had proved invalid, and a consequent muddle over a marriage to Violet Hunt that could not be recognised under British law. Hueffer went to Germany. To cap everything, he lost some of Lawrence's manuscripts and denied ever having seen them.

Fortunately, as Hueffer faded out of Lawrence's life, another influential man of letters took his place. Edward Garnett wrote inquiring about possible stories for an American magazine. Lawrence's stories proved unsuitable, but a friendship developed. That autumn Lawrence spent several week-ends at the Garnetts' country home in Kent. Garnett, middle-aged and prosperous, saw the young man's promise and saw, too, the importance of his writing as he felt impelled to write. 'Follow the gleam,' he counselled. All very well, Lawrence commented to Jessie when he told her, all very well for a man of his age and established position, 'but when you're young it's not always easy to know what *is* the gleam.'

He was weary of teaching, tired of his Croydon lodgings. He toyed with the notion of trying journalism, a gamble unlikely to please Louie. Then, in November, a bad cold developed into pneumonia, in those days all too often a killing disease. A telegram brought Ada rushing to his bedside. It was a long time before he was out of danger. Ada had to read Louie's letters to him. Louie herself came down for Christmas, by which time he was really on the mend. Jessie too made the long journey to see him, staying with Helen Corke. They sat by the fire in his bedroom, the winter sunshine streaming through the window, and talked as they had not talked since his mother's funeral. He inquired about the notes she was making to help with his novel, and said he would like to have them on his next visit to Nottingham.

First, though, the doctor insisted on a month's convalescence. Lawrence went off to Bournemouth where, even in January, the sea air and the fragrant pinewoods would be good for his lungs. Those lungs, the doctor warned him, might become tubercular if he returned to teaching. Lawrence could not afford to resign his post, so, for the time being, he merely asked for sick leave.

He enjoyed life in the big comfortable boarding-house. Besides the usual high proportion of elderly ladies there were some young people, 'quite gay'. But, he teased Louie, 'I do not flirt with the girls – there are some very pretty –

83

only with the old, old maids.' He played cards and other games in the recreation-room, walked in the soft Hampshire countryside, and took several drives (quite a novelty for him, in 1912) in the 'big motor car belonging to the establishment'. Gazing out over the English Channel, he felt the stir of 'wanderlust'. He had received, through his aunt's German sister-in-law, an invitation to visit Cologne at Easter.

As strength returned, he worked on *The Trespasser*. He would have to persuade Helen to release him from his promise not to publish it for five years. The boarding-house had provided him with a comfortable room and a blazing fire. He could be sociable or solitary as he pleased. He enjoyed the regular lavish meals, the excursions, tea 'out' at one of the 'lovely restaurants', gin and bitters before dinner. Life had never been so well ordered, so relaxed. He surrendered to its luxurious cosiness, but by the beginning of February he was more than ready to leave. Under his deceptive calm, behind the social smile he turned on his fellow-guests, emotions were stirring.

Garnett had invited him to Kent. Passing through London, he arranged to meet Helen at Victoria Station. They had tea together and she agreed that he might publish *The Trespasser* as soon as he liked. They talked lightly, without drama, but she knew that he would never return to Croydon and that probably she would never see him again. And so it proved.

Farewells were in the air. He had not written to Louie for a week. The next day, sitting in Garnett's house, he sent her a letter breaking off their engagement. It was an embarrassed, feeble composition, filled with inconsistent excuses. His doctors had advised him not to marry, 'at least for a long time, if ever'. Ada said it was unfair to Louie to hold her. 'My health is so precarious, I wouldn't undertake the responsibility.' Having struck this attitude of honourable self-sacrifice, Lawrence spoiled the effect by saying that they were not 'well suited'. His illness had changed him, and 'broken a good many of the old bonds'.

Louie wrote back suggesting further consideration. Would he telegraph at once? Instead, he wrote a brief letter. He did not think now that he had 'the proper love to marry on'. He went home a few days later and they met in Nottingham. They went up on the Castle Rock, desperately talking out their situation, Louie laughing and crying by turns. She felt she had made herself cheap. Now she was aggressive (Lawrence reported to Garnett) and 'ikey', the Nottinghamshire dialect term for high and mighty. 'If she'd been wistful, tender and passionate,' he confessed, 'I should have been a goner.' They went down into the city to a restaurant, and then parted for ever.

It was easier now for him to visit Jessie. He took her a box of chocolates, a conventional gesture quite out of character. Jessie too was nervous. She found a defence in knitting, until he remarked sarcastically, 'There's nothing I admire like industry,' and she felt unable to do another stitch. He was in a bitter mood. She let him talk on. Suddenly he said:

'If we were to get married now, you'd expect me to stay at home.'

She agreed, pointing out reasonably enough that home was where one worked.

'I don't want a home,' he said. 'I want to be free. I think I shall go abroad.' He told her of the invitation to Germany. He would like, he said, to wander on from there and spend a whole year away. She thought it was a good idea. He had now sent in his resignation from his Croydon post, but he could always return to teaching if he was forced to. But he was not putting forward this foreign scheme with any single-minded confidence – she could tell

that, as so often, his mind was a tug-of-war between con-
flicting desires. She felt deeply sorry for him and slipped
her hand into his.

It was time for his train home. She gave him the notes
she had promised, to help with his novel, and went to
see him off at the station. On the electric tram, rattling
and lurching down the city's hilly roads, it was his turn to
seize her hand. 'I wish,' he said, 'we could run away on this.'

Very soon he was sending her, a few pages at a time, the
new version of the Paul Morel story and she was delighted
to see that all his old power and spontaneity had come
back. The first chapters showed that her criticisms had
been justified. Now, she felt sure, he would produce the
novel she had wanted him to write. At the same time he
was correcting the proofs of *The Trespasser*. Heinemann's had not much cared for it, so he had taken it to
the firm of Duckworth's, with which Garnett was connected. The book would be out in May – production was
much faster in that era – but it was unlikely to earn him
much money.

So February passed into March. Between bouts of white-
hot writing he liked to escape and visit Jessie's sister, May,
now married and living in a cottage close by. His own
sister, he complained, was all set to take over their
mother's possessive role. If he went out, she pestered him
with questions, 'Where have you been? Who did you
meet?' Ada must not think, he said grimly, that she was
his mother.

He went into Nottingham to visit the Chambers family.
Jessie's mother welcomed him as in the old days, though
she was strongly against him as a son-in-law. Mr Chambers made it quietly clear that Lawrence had gone down in
his estimation. Nothing could ever restore the atmosphere
of the old farm at the Haggs. Lawrence himself had
changed, and knew it.

86

The new novel was completed by the middle of March. The fresh version had taken just six weeks. As Jessie received the later chapters her original delight withered. The literary quality was still there, but the truth of the picture had gone. In her eyes Lawrence's integrity had proved unequal to the task. 'The break came in the treatment of Miriam', the treatment of herself. Miriam's part in Paul's artistic development – her own, that is, in Lawrence's – was not given its due significance. She realised with horror that his mother's supremacy was still potent even after death. Even in the novel Mrs Lawrence must be given the victory.

It was the death-blow to their friendship. She made no comment, but Lawrence began posting the sections of manuscript to her instead of taking them in personally. It was ironical. In urging him to stick to the truth she had produced a result she herself shied away from as unacceptable. She saw Lawrence as dishonest and disloyal, making the story develop as it did. The opposite view might have been argued against her.

During March Lawrence paid a visit to George Neville, the old schoolfellow whose hurried marriage had driven him into exile in Staffordshire. He asked George how he felt about the baby whose arrival had caused so much trouble. Nothing, said his friend, nothing at all. Lawrence reported the conversation to Jessie and May when he returned home. 'Fatherhood's a myth,' he said. 'There's nothing in it.' The young women did not try to argue with him. It was obvious that Lawrence, having broken one engagement, was unlikely to rush into another. 'The average man with a family,' he told them, 'is nothing but a cart-horse, dragging the family behind him for the best part of his life. I'm not going to be a cart-horse.'

He had always been dogmatic. Nowadays he seemed to feel that he had almost a divine mission. Yet there were still flashes of the old humorous Lawrence. He would mimic the affectations of the literary people he had mixed with in London. This time, coming from a tiresome cross-country journey in slow Sunday trains, he amused them with imitations of a theatrical touring company he had travelled with. Later, this chance encounter contributed material to his novel, *The Lost Girl*. No experience, however brief, was ever wasted on Lawrence.

The next day he suggested a walk with Jessie. They took the path through the old hay-fields. Lawrence said there must be violets in the hedgerows, he had seen the pit-lads carrying bunches home. At last he braced himself and asked, outright, for any comments she might have to make on the manuscript.

'I've put some notes in with it,' she said, and he did not press her to say more. They went back to May's cottage and had tea. She gave him the parcel. Then it was time for her to cycle back to Nottingham. He said he would walk with her to the top of the hill. Jessie did not want to be alone with him and asked May to come too. So it was with the elder sister that Lawrence turned back when they had said goodbye. 'She's wild with me, isn't she?' he said. 'She's angry about something.' But May seemed to have been told nothing – Jessie was secretive and May never probed with questions – so he got no enlightenment there.

More and more, now, he was thinking of Germany and how a long stay abroad could be arranged. Perhaps he could get a post as *lektor* in some university, teaching English to students? The work would be far lighter than teaching boys in Croydon. He would need advice and recommendations from the University College in Nottingham.

The obvious person to approach was that Professor

Weekley whose elegant manner had so impressed him in his student days. The Professor, as a young man, had been a *lektor* himself. He had found his wife in Germany.

Weekley was cordial. He asked Lawrence to lunch at his home in Mapperley, a residential suburb near the Chambers' farm. Lawrence was welcomed by Mrs Weekley, a tall blonde woman, much younger than her husband, looking indeed not much older than Lawrence himself. She had high cheekbones and striking eyes, green flecked with brown. She exuded vitality. She could have taken the stage as a heroine in one of Wagner's operas.

Lawrence walked after her into the drawing-room, and, in that instant, walked out of the first half of his life and into the second.

7   THE RUNAWAYS

What kind of a bird was this?

That, she confessed later, was the question in Frieda Weekley's mind as she listened to the pale, thin young teacher with the reddish moustache and rather shrill, emphatic flow of words. She was amused, and intrigued, that within a few minutes of entering her house he was holding forth about the impossibility of women. He had finished with them, he announced, and with any further effort to understand them.

She wondered what his experience of women had been. She knew he had written a novel and some poetry, so there must be something about him different from the common run of her husband's students. She was bored with the placid routine of her own life. Of late she felt only half alive. This extraordinary young man had magnetism and she responded.

Frieda was the daughter of a German aristocrat, Baron von Richthofen. The family owned lands and a small castle. Her relatives had included ambassadors, statesmen and a famous explorer. Frieda, as a girl, had known the glitter of the social season in imperial Berlin. At a palace ball the Kaiser himself had remarked on her beauty and asked who she was. The Richthofens had brains as well as looks. Frieda's elder sister took a doctorate in social economics. Frieda herself had intellectual tastes and held the shocking modern view that the sexes were equal.

At nineteen she had met Weekley at a Black Forest holiday-resort. He was fifteen years older, but he had the scholarly aura of four great universities, Cambridge, London, Paris and Berne. He wore too the quiet dignity then widely envied as the hallmark of the English gentleman. Within the year they were married.

Over the next twelve years she learned, sadly, that perfect manners were not enough. There was not, behind that British reserve, the fervent passion she had hoped to find. They had children, a son Montague, two daughters Elsa and Barbara, but much as she loved them they could not fill her life. The marriage proved humdrum, the College a little backwater, not even an independent university. Weekley, for all his brilliance, seemed content to settle there, not treat it as a stepping-stone. As things turned out, he remained for forty years. Nottingham was a city of hard-headed lace-manufacturers and other businessmen. She missed the cultural and social life she had tasted briefly as a girl. Frustrated, hot-blooded, she risked a few slight love-affairs to break the monotony, but by the time she met Lawrence she had virtually given up. She was a reluctant suburban wife, sleep-walking through the best years of her womanhood.

From this condition Lawrence startled her into wakefulness. They talked with animation. The Professor faded into the background, the object of Lawrence's visit became almost unimportant. Lunch was cleared, they talked on through the afternoon. Dusk fell. Outside, the lamplighter went by with his tall pole, looping necklaces of yellow twinkling gas along the hillside roads and crescents. At last Lawrence tore himself away and, in no mood for catching prosaic trains, tramped the eight miles through the cool spring darkness to Eastwood.

Mere good manners required a thank-you letter to his hostess, but hardly one telling her she was 'the most wonderful woman in all England'. On Easter Sunday he paid a second visit. She offered him tea, but the maids were out and she had to confess that, after twelve years of married life, she still did not know how to light the gas under the kettle. Lawrence was horrified. He also rebuked her bluntly for her attitude to the Professor. 'You're quite unaware of your husband. You take no notice of him.'

Despair may have accentuated his roughness. At this stage his situation must have seemed without hope. He had just met a woman he could really love – and she was beyond his reach. The next day, April 8, was a public holiday. He caught the train into Nottingham with Ada and her fiancé to go to a music-hall. Jessie was at the station, meeting May. She caught a glimpse of Lawrence off guard, before he noticed her. His misery was beyond anything she had ever imagined.

That mood did not last. There were further meetings with Frieda. Weekley was wrapped up in his own academic interests. It was the year he published his book, *The Romance of Words*. He seemed unconscious that another kind of romance was developing under his nose.

Lawrence met Frieda and the two little girls for a country walk. Elsa and Barbara ran to and fro, long-legged and coltish in their pink-and-white striped frocks, leaving the two adults to talk undisturbed. But Lawrence, always good with children, was quite ready to play with them. They found a little stream rushing along under a stone bridge. He made them paper boats. 'The Spanish Armada – and you don't know what *that* was,' he challenged them. 'Yes, we *do*!' protested Elsa who was nearly ten. He struck matches and turned the paper boats into Drake's fire ships. They screamed with excitement and delight.

Frieda soon made it plain that her feelings for Lawrence matched his own. There was more than mere physical desire. Each felt that the other was the inevitable mate, indispensable for future happiness. Lawrence had little to lose. Frieda, with husband, home, children, social position, had almost everything. Yet she was the reckless one. Weekley was away one Sunday and she invited Lawrence to stay the night with her. Lawrence refused. He might deride the old-fashioned conventions and rail against bourgeois society but his sense of honour was strict. If Frieda was unhappy in her marriage and determined to end it, fair enough – let her run away with him. But he would not sleep with her under her husband's roof.

It was a fortunate coincidence that she too was planning a visit to Germany. There was to be a great family gathering of the Richthofens at Metz, where the Baron's old regiment was putting on a celebration for the fiftieth anniversary of his entering the German army. It was natural that, for such an occasion, Frieda should travel without her English husband. It was convenient that Lawrence's long-discussed journey would be timed for the same period. Whatever Fate held in store for them later, the two lovers should be able to snatch a few days together without risk of discovery.

For the next week or two Lawrence had to keep his secret. He could not help talking about Frieda – he did so to May – but he dared not reveal what he had in mind.

Only to Garnett, far away in London, was it safe to speak. He wanted Garnett to meet Frieda. 'She is ripping,' he wrote, 'she's the finest woman I've ever met.' A week later she was going to London. Lawrence went at the same time. He had various people to see, including Walter de la Mare, whose reputation as a poet was established that year by the publication of *The Listeners*. He took Frieda to meet Garnett. It must have been an animated encounter, for Frieda left behind part of the *Paul Morel* manuscript and Lawrence forgot his gloves.

They planned their departure for the following week. Lawrence went back to Eastwood to complete his preparations. An Englishman then needed no passport or other travel documents. His gold sovereigns made him welcome everywhere. Lawrence unfortunately had only eleven pounds sterling, but in 1912 even that sum, with care, would carry him some way.

He stayed for the last week-end with May and her husband near Eastwood. On the Sunday morning Jessie and her father drove over unexpectedly with the horse and trap. She noted that Lawrence had lost his despairing look, but seemed 'tongue-tied'. She gathered that he was off to Germany within the week, but she had no idea that he was not going alone.

It is small wonder that Lawrence was preoccupied. The next day, Frieda was to tell her husband that she was leaving him. Lawrence had insisted on that. Now he was on tenterhooks, wondering what Weekley would say.

Jessie asked if he would care to drive home with them. He explained that he had promised to stay at her sister's. He would ride some of the way, though, and walk back across the fields. He climbed into the trap with her and Mr Chambers, who maintained his cool manner towards the young man he had once admired so much. Jessie inquired about Lawrence's writing. He spoke of a play, *The Widowing of Mrs Holroyd*, that Garnett was trying to place for him. Nothing was said of the novel that had caused such dissension between them. They reached the hilltop where he must turn back. Mr Chambers reined in the horse. He hoped Lawrence would enjoy better health in the future. There were polite handshakes all round. Lawrence jumped down into the road. He looked after them, hat raised, as they drove round the next bend, Jessie waving. They never met again.

During the previous year Jessie had been quietly writing a novel that gave her own version of their relationship. She first called it *The Rathe Primrose*, then (after the heroine's name) *Eunice Temple*. She destroyed the manuscript, but when in 1935 she published her memories in *D. H. Lawrence: A Personal Record* she disguised her identity under the mystifying initials 'E. T.'.

Lawrence was now looking forward, not back. He made his family farewells and set off for London. There Frieda joined him as arranged. She had left her son with his father. Elsa and Barbara she delivered to their Weekley grandparents in Hampstead. Her tumultuous emotions are barely imaginable. She was not an unloving mother. The separation tore her apart and continued to do so. That she could set her teeth and go through with the plan is a measure of the power exerted by this young man she had met only a few weeks before.

On May 3 they caught the train from Charing Cross Station to Dover, and boarded the Ostend steamer with the usual tourist crowd of the period, the tweedy gentlemen and their ladies, hatted and veiled and long-skirted, with their masses of luggage and their plaid rugs to protect them from the wind. Lawrence too looked very English in his cloth cap and raincoat. The crossing took three or four hours. He and Frieda sat on deck, 'full' (she

95

recalled) 'of hope and agony', while the leaden waters of the North Sea slid past the rail.

Landing in Belgium, they went on by train to Metz, a strongly fortified garrison-town which the Germans had taken from the French in 1870. It was the city of Frieda's childhood. Her parents lived just outside, in a pleasant house with a walled garden. Fortunately, because of the Baron's military jubilee, the house was bursting with relations from all over Germany, so Frieda had a good excuse to book into a hotel. Even there she found her younger sister, Johanna or 'Nusch', then 'at the height of her beauty and elegance'. Nusch took to the odd Englishman at sight. Within minutes she had sized him up and whispered to Frieda, 'You can go with him. You can trust him.' Frieda confided in her elder sister too, but to her parents, absorbed in the family reunion, she said nothing of Lawrence. She could not conceal from them, however, that her marriage was breaking up.

For Lawrence those first days with his beloved were anything but blissful. Frieda was involved all day with her relatives. Left to his own devices, he walked among the vineyards clothing the hillsides, or sat in the hotel struggling to concentrate on the revision of *Paul Morel*. Apart from the boredom, he felt strangled by the lies into which he had been forced. These, however, were brought to an end by a farcical mishap.

He and Frieda, in a rare hour snatched together, were lying on the grass near the fortifications. Far from showing the slightest interest in ramparts and gun-emplacements, Lawrence was talking earnestly and twisting the old emerald ring on Frieda's finger. But the murmur of voices in English was enough. It was 1912, and the threat of the first World War already clouded the horizon. A zealous policeman advanced and Lawrence was arrested.

'They vow I am an English officer – *I* – *I*!! The damn

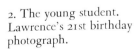

1. The Lawrences. Emily, George and Ernest behind; Ada, Mrs Lawrence, Bert and Mr Lawrence in front.

2. The young student. Lawrence's 21st birthday photograph.

3. Lawrence in 1913, the year of *Sons and Lovers*.

4. Lawrence's possessive mother. While she lived, no girl had a chance to hold his love.

5. The two contrasting worlds of Lawrence's Nottinghamshire boyhood. (i) 'I shall never forget the Haggs' – the farm depicted in *Sons and Lovers*. (ii) Brinsley Colliery, where his father worked.

6. 'Women in love' – powerful influences on Lawrence's life and work.

(i) Jessie Chambers, 'Miriam' in *Sons and Lovers*.

(ii) Louie Burrows, 'Ursula' in *The Rainbow*.

(iii) Helen Corke, whose tragic affair with another man inspired *The Trespasser*.

(iv) Frieda von Richthofen, wife of Professor Ernest Weekley.

7. Katherine Mansfield, the
brilliant New Zealand
short-story writer, in 1912.

8. John Middleton Murry,
man of letters, in 1912.

9. Fontana Vecchia, at
Taormina in Sicily.
Lawrence's home from
1920 to 1923.

Dorothy Brett, one of
[Lawr]ence's most devoted
[discip]les, who followed him
[to N]ew Mexico.

11. Mabel Dodge Sterne,
later Luhan, 'a woman
who liked her own way'.

12. View from Lawrence's ranch in New Mexico, where he vainly
sought escape from materialistic civilization. Taos lies hidden in the
valley.

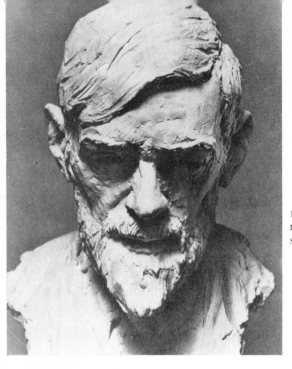

13. The dying Lawrence in ▶
modelled by the American
sculptor, Jo Davidson.

14. Still from the film, *The Virgin and the Gypsy*. Many of
Lawrence's works have been adapted as films or plays.

fools,' he wrote to Garnett. Frieda had to go to her father. It needed 'all the fiery little Baron von Richthofen's influence' to obtain his release. After that, Frieda could not avoid taking Lawrence to tea with her parents, and that worldly-wise couple drew their own conclusions about the relationship. To satisfy the police (and perhaps the Baron too) Lawrence had to quit Metz. He went to Trier and then to his aunt's German in-laws at the tiny village of Waldbröl in the Rhineland. Not till May 24 was he re-united with Frieda, and they were able to begin a week of real 'honeymoon' in the Bavarian Alps.

There they would sit at breakfast in the hotel garden under great horsechestnut trees whose pink and white flowers drifted silently down upon the table. Far below, the river raced over a weir, jade-green from the glaciers, with lumber-rafts bumping on its surface. The lovers took long walks into the mountains and forests. The flowers, Lawrence wrote to Willie Hopkin's wife at Eastwood, were 'so many they would make you cry for joy.' To this old friend he confided that he 'never knew what love was before.' The world was 'wonderful and beautiful and good beyond one's wildest imagination.' Life *could* be great, he declared exultantly, 'quite god-like.'

For most of June and July they were lent, through Frieda's sister, a four-room flat with a balcony on the upper floor of a chalet in the Isar valley. Here Lawrence wrote some of his poems, such as 'River Roses':

> By the Isar, in the twilight
> We were wandering and singing ...

But it was not all roses, not all singing.

Weekley bombarded Frieda with letters, imploring her to come back. The children were missing her. Frieda was missing them. She was in all things a woman of

97

powerful passions, not confined to sexual love. Her laughter was gusty, her temper quick and terrible. Now, in some moods, she would lie on the floor in abandoned misery, at once in love with Lawrence and furious with him. She wanted him to beg of her, 'Stay for my sake.' And he would not, his own strange integrity prevented him. He loved her. In his heart he felt that if she did leave him he could not live for six months without her. But he would not say so. 'Decide what you want most,' he forced himself to tell her, 'to live with me and share my rotten chances, or go back to security and your children ... choose for *yourself*.'

Weekley refused to divorce her. Divorce in 1912 was rare among respectable English people of the middle class. The very word, like 'cancer', was to be whispered. Divorce could ruin a man's career and turn a woman into a social outcast. Weekley was a chivalrous man. It was largely for Frieda's sake that he would agree to no more than a legal separation, which would tone down the scandal and enable her to see the children when she went back to England. But it would not allow her to marry Lawrence, and, as the latter wrote to Mrs Hopkin, 'Oh, if only people could marry properly; I believe in marriage.'

Mrs Hopkin was one of the few people, still, in whom he could confide. In Nottinghamshire the affair was something to be hushed up. Of his own relatives only Ada knew – and she, herself about to be married, was deeply shocked and embittered by what he had done. Jessie too he had told, thinking it would help her to forget him. She did in fact marry another school-teacher three years later. Louie Burrows he did not tell until November, though even then he did not reveal Frieda's name. 'The best thing you can do is to hate me,' he told Louie in a remorseful letter for the way he had treated

98

her. Louie did not marry until 1940, when she had almost completed her successful career as a headmistress. Neither woman ever quite got over her association with Lawrence. No one did. He was a man to leave scars, though even the scars were often treasured.

So the runaways stayed together, and if Weekley or any one else had expected the affair to turn out a fleeting infatuation the passage of the months proved otherwise. Lawrence and Frieda were right for each other, and that rightness went far beyond the mere satisfactions of physical love. That Frieda was six years his senior did not matter, and was indeed an asset, for it differentiated her from the girls he had known and provided that maternal quality in a woman for which he would always hunger. Frieda helped him, as no one else could, to throw off at last the dead hand of his mother.

She would not, like the girls, be dominated. In turn she would not – the thing he had always dreaded – dominate him. They stood up to each other. Their tempestuous rows were to become famous. They did not stop at words, they threw crockery. But their very quarrels often arose from love. Neither could bear the other to lapse from the high level normally expected and admired. If Lawrence seemed for a moment to be surrendering his artistic integrity, Frieda loved him enough to be furious. And if Frieda, the emancipated modern woman, slipped back into some snobbish conventional prejudice unworthy of her, Lawrence was so disappointed that he must stamp (though not literally) on his idol's feet of clay.

There were money difficulties in those first months. Lawrence had to write for an advance on *The Trespasser*. At one point he had only four pounds. There was reluctant talk of his trying to get some lecturing in Munich when the autumn came, but before then his publishers had sent him fifty pounds. Living was cheap if they did their own house-keeping. Frieda could not cook the simplest meal. There had always been servants. It was lucky that Lawrence possessed the domestic skills. He had to teach her.

In August they took rucksacks and walked over the mountains into Austria. One night they were stranded at the top of a pass and had to sleep in a hay-hut. They spent a month at the Tyrolean village of Mayrhofen, lodging at a farm. The valley was overhung by high mountains, capped with eternal snow. The air was loud with tinkling cow-bells and the thunder of waterfalls. Frieda would undress and sun-bathe. Sometimes they braved the icy streams. They made picnic lunches, ate the local cheese and eggs boiled over a camp-fire. At night they drank with the villagers and danced.

They decided to go south before winter came. In September they walked over the Brenner Pass and down to Riva at the head of Lake Garda, still in Austria, which lost this territory only after the first World War. A few miles down the lake they crossed the frontier, and found a flat in Gargnano, a waterside village that could be reached only by steamer. It cost a little over three English pounds per month, 'everything supplied,' he told Garnett, 'everything nice ... clean as a flower'. Lawrence fell in love with Italy and the simple solid values of the people. 'What does it matter if one is poor?' he challenged an old Croydon colleague. 'One *can* have the necessary things, life, and love, and clean warmth. Why is England so shabby?'

By mid-November he had finished *Paul Morel* and sent it to London. 'I tell you I have written a great book,' he assured Garnett earnestly. Posterity has endorsed his claim. For once he had made a real effort to prune and shape his work. 'I tell you it has got form – *form*,' he insisted. 'Haven't I made it patiently, out of sweat as well as blood?' Later in this well-known letter, in which he explains his own idea of the theme and tries to forestall criticism, he emphasises: 'I *have* patiently and laboriously constructed that novel.' It was not wasted effort. The book came out early in the following summer, retitled *Sons and Lovers*, and for many readers will always remain the most satisfying, artistically, of all the novels he wrote. Yet the publishers lost money on the first edition. As for his *Love Poems*, which had come out a few months earlier, the initial sales were negligible. As so often, genius had to be nursed slowly into success.

Lawrence was always inclined to lose interest in his books once they were printed. His creative energy spurred him on to the tasks ahead. *Sons and Lovers*, though in some respects a milestone in the English fiction of that time, belonged also to the nineteenth-century tradition in which Lawrence had grown up. Now that he had made his own contribution to that tradition he was ready to move on into fresh fields.

It was during this first year or two with Frieda that he began to develop some of the ideas most characteristic of his later work. More and more strongly he was coming to feel that modern man had erred in placing so much reliance on reason. 'We can go wrong in our minds,' he declared. 'But what our blood feels and believes and says, is always true.' For all his wide reading he seems not to have encountered the ideas of the psychologist Freud until Frieda introduced them to him, but he had begun groping his way independently to a realisation of the part played by the unconscious. He never became – as some critics mistakenly but understandably imagined – an enemy of reason. He simply felt that too many people had exalted reason as the only important factor and it was up to him to correct the balance by emphasising the 'dark forces' of the blood. Like Freud, he was to be criticised for explaining everything in terms of sex. In reality, Lawrence was passionately interested in many other aspects of life, but once more he felt it to be his mission to correct the balance. He would write and talk about sex because, up to that date, scarcely any one had dared to, especially in the English language. The humbug and hypocrisy and the false shame must be swept away. Then people would be able to see Life clearly in perspective.

The sense of mission that May had detected was growing stronger and more definite. 'I've something here,' he told a friend in 1913, striking his chest with a sudden violent gesture, 'that is heavier than concrete. If I don't get it out, it will kill me.'

Before that, during the winter at Gargnano, he had begun a long work, *The Sisters*, which eventually became two related novels, *The Rainbow* and *Women in Love*. Once more he drew heavily on his own experiences – 'Ursula' was modelled on Louie – but the style was changing. He knew, as the story evolved, that Garnett would not like it. Garnett admired contemporary novelists such as Joseph Conrad, John Galsworthy and Arnold Bennett, writers in the great tradition. As the new work proceeded, cracks gradually appeared in the old sympathetic relationship with Garnett. By 1914 Lawrence was writing to him, 'It is no good unless you will have patience and understand what I *want* to do. I am not after all a child working erratically.'

Frieda encouraged him in his change of outlook. 'You are fighting the old standards,' she told him, 'breaking new ground.' And many years afterwards she defended herself: 'They say I ruined Lawrence's genius, but I know it is not so.'

In June, 1913, however, when they paid a short visit

to England so that Frieda could see her children, the link with Garnett was still close, and they stayed with him and his family. Constance Garnett was famous as a translator of Russian literature, and their own son David, then twenty-one and already very friendly with Lawrence and Frieda, was to become eminent as an imaginative writer.

Lawrence was now greatly widening his acquaintance. People were eager to meet the author of *Sons and Lovers*, which was being extensively reviewed and praised. He formed a friendship with the son and daughter-in-law of the then Prime Minister, Mr Asquith. Herself later the author of novels, memoirs and children's books, Lady Cynthia Asquith seemed to Frieda 'lovely as Botticelli's Venus'. Lawrence admired her immensely and corresponded with her for the rest of his life. She was 'always a loyal friend,' said Frieda, 'even through the war, when friends were rare.' Their introduction to the Asquiths was made by Edward Marsh, a generous promoter of young poets, who was then working under Winston Churchill at the Admiralty.

The new friendship, however, which was to mean most in their lives was made with a young couple, John Middleton Murry and Katherine Mansfield, who were in the same plight as themselves, deeply in love but unable yet to marry, since Katherine was awaiting a divorce. She was a New Zealander, still only twenty-four. Frieda found her 'the perfect friend ... so exquisite and complete, with her fine brown hair, delicate skin, and brown eyes.' Lawrence (though capable of unkindness to her in later years) was no less attracted, depicting her in *Women in Love* as 'so *charming*, so infinitely charming, in her softness and in her fine, exquisite richness of texture and delicacy of line.' She had already published her first volume of short stories, *In a German Pension*, and was to win, in her tragically brief life, a remarkable reputation in that literary form.

Jack Murry, whose own field was to be that of critic and biographer, was a journalist recently down from Oxford. He was editing a little magazine, *Rhythm*, for which Katherine was writing. Grey-eyed and good-looking, with a broad smile, he too appealed to Frieda. 'I fell for Katherine and Murry,' she said, 'when I saw them quite unexpectedly on the top of a bus, making faces at each other and putting their tongues out.'

Katherine was a sympathetic ally in carrying messages between Frieda and her children, who were still living with their grandparents and attending school in Hampstead. Direct contact was proving difficult. One morning Frieda intercepted them. They hugged her and demanded when she was coming back. But they must have mentioned the encounter and been forbidden to speak to her. At the next meeting the little white faces looked silently back at her, as if she were an evil spirit. Weekley seemed implacable. He was a Christian gentleman as his generation understood the phrase. He had offered to take Frieda back and forgive her adultery, but if she stayed with Lawrence he could not have his children contaminated by her. His rigid code had no room for the sort of compassion that both mother and children needed. Lawrence himself, rather curiously, retained a great respect for this man, so different from himself.

He and Frieda left England again in August. She went to see her parents in Germany. He walked through Switzerland and over the St Gotthard Pass. They met in Milan and moved south to a little fishing village on the Italian Riviera, overlooking the gulf where Shelley had drowned almost a century earlier. There they stayed for eight months, trying vainly to get the Murrys to come out and join them. But they were not lonely. Lawrence's growing literary reputation impressed the local British residents – the Consul and his wife typed his manuscripts, and even the chaplain (not knowing the scandal of their unmarried state) was all affability. Edward Marsh and other literary figures appeared from the great world outside. In London there was the beginning of the Lawrence cult. Young writers like Rebecca West, Viola Meynell and Ivy Low, became his enthusiastic champions against what they saw as the indifference or faint praise of the established giants.

Recognition was welcome, but Lawrence needed money too. Small cheques dribbled in. He was unlucky in his American publisher of *Sons and Lovers*. Not a dollar reached him, and ten years later he was still lamenting that America had read his most popular book for nothing. Over that whole period his total income barely equalled what he would have earned as a teacher.

Weekley at last faced the truth that Frieda meant to stay with her lover. He opened proceedings and, late in May of the following year, 1914, the divorce was granted. Lawrence and Frieda hurried to London and stayed in Kensington, where they were quietly married at the local register office on July 13. Murry and Katherine were witnesses. On their way to the ceremony, Lawrence hastily bought a wedding-ring, and Frieda gave her old one to Katherine. It lies buried with her at Fontainebleau, where she died in 1923, still only thirty-four, after a long battle with tuberculosis.

The Lawrences were now respectable. Frieda could accompany her new husband to stay with his sister, Ada, who now lived in Derbyshire. Problems like that were eased, but Frieda was still cut off from her children. All she was permitted was a strained half-hour meeting in a lawyer's office.

Otherwise, things were looking up. Lawrence was

becoming known. Literary groups competed for his support. Marsh had gathered round him a band of poets whose work he published in annual volumes entitled *Georgian Poetry*, after the new king, George V. These 'Georgian' poets included the future laureate, John Masefield, together with Robert Graves, W. H. Davies, Walter de la Mare, and Rupert Brooke, whom Lawrence met that June at Marsh's lunch-table, and who was to die within the year on the ill-fated Dardanelles expedition.

Lawrence was often claimed as a Georgian, though he disliked labels. His subject-matter was not dissimilar. The Georgians were much concerned with landscape and Nature and with intense personal emotions – the lesser versifiers might fall into mere prettiness, but the best of them achieved poignant beauty, or 'loveliness', to use a word then favoured and one which Lawrence himself used. Where he differed from the Georgians was in technique. They went in for rhymes and regular rhythms and even for the most elaborate verse-forms such as the sonnet and the rondel. To Lawrence this was all too artificial and meant death to spontaneity. '*Skilled* poetry,' he told Edward Marsh, 'is dead in fifty years.' His own best poems, he insisted, came from a kind of haunting 'demon' inside him, which defied taming and 'makes his own form willy-nilly, and is unchangeable.' His poems must rush out as this demon determined. They were, as the critic W. E. Williams says, 'detonated rather than composed'. The results are uneven in merit. Lawrence, or the 'demon' within him, was amazingly prolific, and not all those hundreds of poems could be first-rate. But in the best of them there is a pulse-beat of emotional power, an intensity of vision and feeling, the characteristic Lawrentian reverence for life, which no reader can miss.

Lawrence's preference for free verse encouraged a rival

group, Ezra Pound's Imagists, in an attempt to enlist him, but he could not really be fitted into that category either. Through them, however, he made friends with Richard Aldington, who was to become better known for his novels and other prose, including a book on Lawrence entitled *Portrait of A Genius, But ...*

During that July London basked in the glow of an age about to pass away for ever. However much he might scorn bourgeois values, Lawrence had escaped from his working-class origins and could share in the illusion of individual liberty and security enjoyed by every middle-class Englishman with a few pounds in his pocket. No one could give him orders. No one could make him serve in the army, show his papers, or ask permission to go about his own business. He belonged to a nation that ruled a quarter of the globe, possessed an invincible navy, and could not imagine being defeated in war.

On July 31 Lawrence began a walking tour in the Lake District with three other men. One, a new acquaintance, was a swarthy, picturesque young Russian-Jewish economist, S. S. Koteliansky, whose radical views made life in London more congenial than Tsarist Russia. 'Kot' was to become a life-long friend. For five days the men tramped happily through that rugged, exquisite countryside. They sang songs, Lawrence plucked white-and-gold water-lilies from a mountain tarn and wreathed them round his hat, Kot intoned strange Hebrew chants, Lawrence fooled about and imitated music-hall acts. Even rain could not damp their spirits. They were happy when they crouched in the lee of the dry-stone walls that dissected the upland pastures.

Meanwhile the world was rushing to disaster, but there were no radio bulletins in those days to tell them, and in the remote hamlets where they slept they may scarcely have seen a newspaper, for it was the week-end preceding a public holiday. Lawrence, indifferent to politics and international quarrels, would have been the last person to inquire for news. So, through that holiday week-end, they rambled through scenes that had scarcely altered since Wordsworth's time, and while they did so the threatening telegrams flashed along the wires of Europe, ambassadors wrung their hands, emperors signed mobilization orders, and battle fleets steamed to their stations.

On Wednesday, August 5, 1914, the friends came down to a small industrial town on the coast and were shocked out of their carefree dream. Since midnight, they learned, England had been at war with Germany. Lawrence's country was fighting Frieda's.

8 THE WAR

The first effect of the war was to produce in Lawrence a numbed feeling, his heart 'cold as a lump of dead earth'. The young men of his generation were rushing to enlist in a wave of patriotic emotion. 'Honour has come back, as a king, to earth,' ran a sonnet by Rupert Brooke, who had gained a commission in the Royal Naval Division and was helping in a forlorn attempt to save the Belgian port of Antwerp from the German advance. Lawrence shared in none of this feeling.

He was neither a patriot nor, like a few idealists, a conscientious objector. Obsessed with his own visions he regarded the war as an intolerable interference with his work. He was only half joking when he told one friend, 'I think I am much too valuable a creature to offer myself to a German bullet ...' Luckily, at that early stage, nobody knowing his poor health record would have expected him to volunteer. He was merely complaining to Garnett in October that 'the war puts a damper on one's own personal movements'; but by January (when the war had not, as so many had confidently predicted, been 'over by Christmas') he lamented to Lady Cynthia Asquith in more serious tones: 'The War finished me: it was the spear through the side of all sorrows and hopes.'

It was a deeply significant remark. Though his major tribulations had yet to come, the war of 1914-1918 *did* finish the original Lawrence. Thereafter he was a different, and to many a less attractive, person. The sense of mission grew more urgent, the manner more arrogant. The metaphor of 'the spear through the side', taken from the Crucifixion story, shows that Lawrence was beginning to see himself as some kind of Messiah with a sacred duty to set people on a new road, away from the materialism and bourgeois morality he despised. Any obstacle was apt to be seen as persecution.

It is easy to understand Lawrence's feelings, less easy to sympathise with him all the way. He was not the only young writer whose first book brought him a miserable financial reward, and not the only man whose career had been wrenched out of its course by the war. Lawrence might have counted many blessings if he had been given to that sort of arithmetic. He was not living – or dying – in the flooded trenches, but occupying a series of country cottages either lent him by friends or rented for small sums. The Royal Literary Fund, which existed to help authors, sent him fifty pounds – not ungenerous for a writer who had been working only three or four years – but he found 'no joy in their tame thin-gutted charity', though he did not return the cheque. He was more grateful for the typewriter sent him by the American poet, Amy Lowell.

Such friends were never lacking. He could not complain that the intellectuals had been slow to recognise him, even though the wider public had been backward in buying his books. He had started with great disadvantages for that period – humble parentage, unromantic occupation as a 'Council school' teacher, and the stigma of a recent divorce case – yet despite these, and having been abroad for much of his short literary career, he was already a well-known figure.

A notable new friend was the eccentric Lady Ottoline Morrell, the Duke of Portland's sister married to a pacifist Member of Parliament. Lady Ottoline had been brought up in a world of gloomy grandeur and philistine values. Bored by the 'huntin', shootin' and fishin'' set, she had turned enthusiastically to the society of literary and artistic people, and become a warm-hearted patroness of the struggling unknown. Uncreative herself, she stimulated those who were. 'Ottoline has moved men's imaginations,' Lawrence wrote, 'and that's perhaps the most a woman can do.'

Before the war, she made her London home, an eighteenth-century house in Bedford Square, Bloomsbury, a rendezvous for intellectuals. It was the closing phase of an era when high incomes, low taxes, and an abundance of servants enabled a woman with her interests to carry on the elegant old tradition of the salon. This tradition she had now transferred to her new country home, Garsington Manor, a Tudor mansion near Oxford, set in five hundred acres of grounds. Lawrence compared 'that wonderful lawn, under the ilex trees' with the idyllic garden in Boccaccio, where a party of cultured Florentines, refugees from the city plague, spent their time telling the stories of the *Decameron*. Peacocks stalked those grounds, the oak panelling within had been painted a peacock blue-green, and Lady Ottoline herself was not unlike a peacock in her bottle-green dress trailing across the sward. She is depicted as Hermione Roddice in *Women in Love* and she was probably Priscilla Wimbush in another novel,

Crome Yellow, by Aldous Huxley, whose friendship with Lawrence began about this time. These were fictitious, rather unkind caricatures, but other writers described her, by name, in no less striking phrases. She reminded Virginia Woolf of a mackerel in an aquarium, but David Garnett saw her as 'extremely handsome: tall and lean, with a large head, masses of dark Venetian red hair ... glacier blue-green eyes, a long straight nose, a proud mouth, and a long jutting-out chin made up her lovely, haggard face.' Every one had an individual view of Lady Ottoline, but no one could be unaware of her.

She did not collect Lawrence just as one more promising young celebrity. She read *The White Peacock* and *Sons and Lovers*, and was filled with nostalgia for the Nottinghamshire countryside where she too had spent her childhood, though in the very different setting of Welbeck Abbey, the ducal 'stately home'. She was delighted to learn from Gilbert Cannan that the Lawrences were then living quite near, in a cottage that had been lent them. A warm and genuine friendship developed between them. Lawrence dropped into the Nottinghamshire dialect she loved to hear again and they 'talked of the lovely wild commons, of Sherwood Forest, of the dark pit villages' they both remembered. They took long walks through the woods and over the downs, and not only did the Lawrences stay amid the splendours of Garsington but Lady Ottoline paid them several return visits, afterwards confessing that one night she was too cold to sleep. But, summing up his 'magnetic gift' for companionship, she wrote: 'I felt when I was with him as if I had really at last found a friend, that I could express myself without reserve, and without fear of being thought silly.'

It was Lady Ottoline who introduced Lawrence to the great philosopher, Bertrand Russell, which led to a close but short-lived friendship between the two men, both rebels in utterly different ways against the established order. What with the brilliant Garsington set, and other contacts, Lawrence's circle widened rapidly. It included composers such as Philip Heseltine, who wrote songs under the pen-name Peter Warlock, and painters like Duncan Grant and Mark Gertler. Grant, a highly-regarded young post-Impressionist, much influenced by Cézanne, did not appeal to Lawrence, who dismissed him and his friend as 'beetles'. He afterwards depicted the artist as Duncan Forbes in *Lady Chatterley's Lover*. He did, however, like Gertler, a dark, handsome young Jew who, like himself, had come up the hard way – born of impoverished parents in the London slums and seeing no pictures in his early life save those of the pavement artists. Gertler was obvious material for a novelist. Lawrence almost certainly used him, transformed into a sculptor, Loerke, in *Women in Love*. Aldous Huxley, in *Crome Yellow*, made him the painter Gombauld, 'a black-haired young corsair ... with flashing teeth and luminous large dark eyes'. Gilbert Cannan planned a whole novel with Gertler's interesting life as its theme.

Cannan was just one of the innumerable writers whom Lawrence knew. They ranged from E. M. Forster to the well-loved children's author, Eleanor Farjeon, from Michael Arlen to Compton Mackenzie, whom Lawrence caricatured in a story, 'The Man Who Loved Islands'. Mackenzie and Cannan were at this date probably the two other most promising young novelists in England. Cannan had been secretary to the dramatist, J. M. Barrie, the creator of *Peter Pan*, and had run off with his actress wife, Mary, and in due course married her. Cannan's early brilliance petered out tragically in a mental home, but Mary remained a life-long friend of the Lawrences.

By the spring of 1915 it was evident that the war was

going to prove grimmer than any one had foreseen. The casualties were appalling. Britain had always managed in the past with a small regular army enlarged with patriotic volunteers. Most of these had died in the mud and barbed wire of Flanders. Lawrence, writing to 'my dear Lady Ottoline', noted that there were government changes and they probably meant conscription. His heart was 'icy cold ... with fear'. In another mood he might write that he 'would like to kill a million Germans – two millions', and then tell her to ignore what he said. He thought the English had gone mad but he blamed the Germans for driving them mad. It would be nice if the Lord sent another flood and drowned the world, but he was honest enough to admit that he would probably want to be Noah.

The notion of an ark, preserving a few of the right people from the evils of a world gone wrong, is one which has often appealed to idealistic writers, and in our day, especially as a consequence of the nuclear bomb, has enjoyed an even wider popularity. The hippy communities of California in the nineteen-sixties and the loose associations of other groups, whether in the heart of big cities or on the road to exotic destinations like Khatmandu – in either case determinedly holding apart from conventional society – are just the more recent examples of a tendency familiar long before Lawrence's generation. They do, however, go a little way to explain why his gospel strikes such a sympathetic chord in the hearts of modern youth. Lawrence would have disagreed violently with some of them – it is unlikely that he would have approved of drug-taking as an escape from material reality, when even anything as passive as Buddhist meditation made so little appeal to his ardent, dynamic nature. But in his revolt against artificial and conventional values, his preaching of a return to primitive simplicity, to instinct and 'the wisdom of the blood' rather than to intellect and rational argument, Lawrence foreshadowed much that was to catch the imagination of young people in later days. From 1915 onwards, Lawrence continually toyed with schemes for founding a little community, whether on an island or in some other remote spot, where he and his disciples could live life as he felt it should be lived. At first it had seemed that Garsington Manor might fill the bill, with Lady Ottoline to preside. Now he saw it must be somewhere far from this war-mad Europe. The first thing was to get out.

An American well-wisher offered him a cottage in Florida. Lady Cynthia helped him to get passports, which had become essential under war-time conditions and were not easy to obtain, especially if one's wife was of German origin. Berths were booked, to sail on November 24, but exactly three weeks before that something happened which upset his plans.

His novel, *The Rainbow*, had come out and certain passages, mild by today's standards, had been criticised by reviewers as indecent. One magazine had called it 'an orgy of sexiness'. So, early in November, the police pounced on the stock of copies in the warehouse, and the publishers, Methuen's, were summoned to court to show reason why the books should not be destroyed as obscene. Lawrence himself was charged with nothing, and, owing to the oddity of the law, had no chance to defend his work. The publishers apologized meekly for issuing it, and the magistrate ordered that the copies be destroyed. So, in effect, Lawrence was publicly condemned for the novel he had written with such faith and enthusiasm, and, though it appeared in America, it was suppressed in his own country.

Anyone working his way through the nearly 500 pages of *The Rainbow* in quest of 'an orgy of sexiness' would be sorely puzzled to find it. Lawrence writes powerfully, if not as plainly as some modern authors, of the sensations of physical love. He indicates (what the Victorians had been ashamed to admit) that these sensations could and should be enjoyed by the woman as much as by the man. Besides preaching this important truth, universally accepted today as vital to a happy relationship, he introduces a homosexual episode and refers once to unspecified 'unnatural acts of sensual voluptuousness'.

This was enough for the magistrate. But a careful reading of the book as a whole suggests that there were other elements, quite unconnected with sex, which made the book unpopular in some quarters. There were eloquent denunciations of industrialized society and the capitalist system. 'The pit matters ... the pit owns every man. The women have what is left.' The characters discussed war and nationality in a manner unlikely to foster patriotism. At the end of 1915, with England fighting for her existence, such a book seemed dangerously subversive.

Lawrence cancelled his sailing until the courtroom battle over *The Rainbow* was decided. Then it was too late. Conscription was coming. No one could leave the country without taking a medical examination to show that he was unfit for the army. It seemed unlikely that Lawrence should pass as fit. For two hours he stood in line at the medical centre, but he had a horror of stripping naked to be peered at by the doctors. A wave of revulsion overcame him, and before his turn was reached he walked out.

Even before the *Rainbow* case he had often ranted against his countrymen. Now, more than ever, he felt persecuted, a prophet rejected by his own people. 'I'll never write another word I mean,' he told Frieda. 'They aren't fit for it.' He kept the reddish beard he had grown during a recent illness. It was a gesture of revolt. Beards were forbidden in the army. Christ was traditionally depicted with one.

The Lawrences moved to Cornwall, 'a bare, forgotten country,' he wrote, 'that doesn't belong to England.' At Zennor, not far from Land's End, they found a simple granite cottage to rent at five pounds a year. Upstairs it had just one big room looking out over the Atlantic, like a ship's state-room. Frieda was able at last to indulge her feminine instinct to build a nest. They washed the walls pale pink and painted the cupboards bright blue. They made the place comfortable with second-hand furniture, ransacking the little town of St Ives for good old-fashioned pieces that the local fishermen were throwing out to replace with tawdrier modern stuff. Frieda was delighted when she picked up a well-made bedstead for a shilling. The cottage gleamed with polished brass and rows of china plates.

The Murrys came down and took the next cottage. They arrived sitting on a cart piled high with all their worldly goods, Katherine looking, Frieda recorded, 'like an emigrant'. Frieda loved Katherine – 'her round eyes', her humour, 'her little jackets, chiefly the one that was black and gold like bees', and the long confidential talks the two women had, sitting in the sun among the foxgloves.

Katherine was less happy. She had never wanted to come to Cornwall, and, whereas Frieda was to look back on 'days of complete harmony between the Murrys and us', the New Zealand girl was disgusted by the violent quarrels between Frieda and Lawrence, and equally embarrassed by their frank displays of affection at other times. It was an uncomfortable quartet, with complex interrelations beneath the surface. Both Lawrence and Frieda were strongly attracted to Murry in their different

117

ways. In Lawrence's case there was an emotional yearning for some kind of symbolic blood-brotherhood, as depicted in *Women in Love*, where the character of Gerald Crich is Murry's personality encased in a quite different bodily exterior, drawn from a Nottinghamshire squire and coal-owner, T. P. Barber. In the same novel Katherine became Gudrun Brangwen, sister to the Ursula modelled on Louie Burrows. For all his bitterness over *The Rainbow*, Lawrence was now working on a sequel, though it was not published until after the war. For the rest he was busy preparing collections of poems, *Amores* and *Look! We Have Come Through!* and a travel book, *Twilight in Italy*. As the titles suggest, these volumes of verse were strongly – and recently – autobiographical. Often Lawrence, who could gaze so steadily at the natural world about him, turns that gaze inward upon himself, as in the longish poem, 'Manifesto', written at Zennor, beginning, 'A woman has given me strength ...'

After a few months Katherine made the excuse that the north coast did not suit her – she certainly hated the wild Atlantic winds – and the Murrys departed to a cottage in the milder south of Cornwall. The friendship was never so close again.

That summer Lawrence was called for medical examination. It meant a night in the army barracks at Bodmin, a glimpse of military life with its shouting and stamping which convinced him that a week of it would kill him. On the morrow came the ignoble parade before the doctors. As expected, they pronounced him 'C3', physically unfit for soldiering. He was urged to find some work that would help the war-effort. He ignored the suggestion and went back to his desk at Zennor. Murry, however, though similarly exempt from joining the army, found clerical work in London at the War Office.

The visit to Bodmin upset Lawrence, though it removed the threat of conscription. What other men would have found merely a tiresome and worrying formality was almost a traumatic experience to one so hypersensitive. But worse was to come.

Any stranger settling in a remote country area arouses the curiosity of the local people. In this case the curiosity was multiplied: there was a war on, the Zennor cottage looked out over the Atlantic where German submarines were sinking British ships, Lawrence (being a writer) appeared to do no real work beyond growing excellent vegetables in his garden, and, worst of all, his wife was a German.

Curiosity, fed by gossip, turned to suspicion. Frieda naturally tried to keep in touch with her mother and sisters (her father had died early in the war) and posted letters to a friend in neutral Switzerland. Eavesdropping neighbours heard the Lawrences singing in a foreign language – some of the songs were indeed German *lieder* but others were Gaelic from the Scottish isles. Once, as Frieda and her husband walked home, their rucksack bulging with a loaf of home-made bread given them by a friend, the coastguards leapt from ambush behind a hedge and accused them of concealing a camera. The wildest of the local rumours said that Frieda supplied food to German submarines. Perhaps the loaf in the rucksack was regarded as evidence. This atmosphere began to get on Lawrence's nerves. Once, in a rare mood of high spirits, Frieda ran along the cliff in the sunshine, her white scarf fluttering in the wind. 'Stop it, you fool!' he shouted. 'They'll think you're signalling to the enemy!'

In October, 1917, the affair went beyond the gossip of suspicious neighbours. An official file had been built up against the Lawrences. Coming home by herself one day, Frieda found that the cottage had been ransacked in their absence. Next morning a khaki-clad captain appeared on the doorstep with two detectives and the local policeman, who was somewhat embarrassed because he had always been on friendly terms with the tenants and had accepted vegetables from their garden. The detectives searched the cottage again. They were much intrigued by an old college notebook full of mysterious diagrams, which in fact referred to botanical specimens not batteries. The detectives were not necessarily as stupid as the angry Lawrences thought them, for only a few years earlier Baden-Powell, the founder of the Scout movement, had spied on the Austrians and used sketches of butterflies to cover his drawings of their defences.

The detectives took possession of some papers, and the army officer produced a document, signed by a general, and read it out. The Lawrences must quit Cornwall within three days, keep out of all 'prohibited areas', and, wherever they settled, report to the nearest police-station.

Lawrence kept calm. 'What is the reason?' he asked.

'You know better than I do.'

Frieda flared up. 'This is your English liberty? Here we live, we don't do anybody any harm, and these creatures –' she gave the detectives a withering look – 'have the right to come and touch our private things?'

'Be quiet,' Lawrence warned her.

They had no choice. They had to obey the expulsion-order. They packed their few possessions and went to London, where Hilda Aldington lent them a room in her flat. It would have been laughable had it not been so serious. Five years earlier the German police had arrested Lawrence as a British spy. Now the British turned him out of his home for the opposite reason.

If, for the rest of his life, he sometimes waxed indignant and almost hysterical about the persecution to which he was subjected. it was not without cause. The suppression of *The Rainbow* and then the eviction from Cornwall were embittering experiences which must never be under-rated in any assessment of his later books and behaviour.

The war dragged on. There was a Communist revolution in Russia, but the other nations continued the struggle, and the United States had now joined the Allies. Would the slaughter never stop? Frieda's heart turned over when she saw her schoolboy son in his cadet uniform. How soon would *he* be called into the trenches?

The Lawrences felt themselves under the eyes of the police. They had to leave the Aldingtons' flat in London. They moved briefly to a cottage in Berkshire near the rolling chalk downs Lawrence liked and used more than once as a setting for his stories. But there was no resting-place there.

They must live somewhere, but they had no money. Frieda ached for home again. Lawrence shrank from acquiring a house or possessions of any kind. He wished he were a fox or a bird. Failing that, he would have liked to get a horse-caravan 'and move on for ever, and never have a neighbour'. Always there was this conflict between their longings.

His sister Ada found them a cottage in Derbyshire, not too far from her own home, and paid a year's rent herself. Mountain Cottage was grandly situated on the rim of a wooded gorge. There, in the very heart of England, no one could accuse them of waving to submarines. Lawrence had to go to Derby for yet another of those medical examinations which most men would have borne with a shrug but which his sensitive temperament exaggerated into an ordeal. He was not, however, ordered to do any kind of war work. Even when he tried to get an office-job, nobody wanted him.

Victory came at last in autumn, 1918, a year after his expulsion from Cornwall. One by one the enemy nations went down like a row of ninepins, Bulgaria, Turkey, Austro-Hungary, then Germany. It was another year before travel restrictions were lifted sufficiently for the Lawrences to cross the Channel again.

Frieda hurried to her family in hungry, defeated Germany. Lawrence arranged to meet her in Italy. He reached Florence on November 19, 1919, after an exhausting series of train journeys across Europe, when he could not afford a sleeping-berth. The author, Norman Douglas, a friend from the old *English Review* days, had booked him a room in a pension overlooking the Arno. There Lawrence waited for Frieda, soaking up material meanwhile which he later used in books.

Frieda arrived two weeks later. He met her off the train at four o'clock in the morning. Italy, the stimulus of Douglas's witty conversation, and the reunion with Frieda herself had combined to restore something of the old high-spirited Lawrence. Though it was December, and fog from the river softened the moonlight, he insisted on bundling her into an open carriage and going for a

123

drive. 'I must show you this town,' he cried with typical intensity. So they trotted through the sleeping streets and along the embankments, with Lawrence pointing out the Ponte Vecchio and Giotto's tower and Michelangelo's David and all the other statues, and Frieda entered into his mood, forgetting the weariness of travel. She thought of Florence ever afterwards as 'the most beautiful town ... the lily town, delicate and flowery'.

Soon they went south, via Rome and Naples, to Capri, where they met another old friend, Compton Mackenzie. Lawrence liked the gay, warm-hearted Scottish novelist, though he criticised his flamboyance – Mackenzie came of a great theatrical family, he had an Oxford sophistication, and his war-service had been adventurous and romantic. He in turn liked Lawrence, though he was amused by his dogmatic manner. It was through Mackenzie's helpfulness that Lawrence found a new publisher, Martin Secker, who was a courageous champion of authors and undertook to bring out *The Rainbow* again and risk another court-case, as well as to take its successor, *Women in Love*, and any future books.

Capri was beautiful, but the island was tiny, only four miles by two, and much of it precipitous, and Lawrence soon felt cramped. The town, 'about as big as Eastwood', with its little square and 'comical whitewashed cathedral', was packed with 'cosmopolitan dwellers – English, American, Russian by the dozen, Dutch, German, Dane'. Lawrence preferred the Italians. Mackenzie was 'a good sort' and they found another old friend there, Mary Cannan, but in the main the artistic and intellectual cliques on Capri seemed to him a 'stew-pot of semi-literary cats'.

Frieda shared his views and was willing to move on. They went to Sicily and took the upstairs half of a spacious farmhouse, Fontana Vecchia, or 'Old Fountain', standing on a rocky hillside just on the outskirts of Taormina. Here they were to spend two happy and productive years. Here he wrote his novels, *The Lost Girl* and *Aaron's Rod*, his poems, *Birds, Beasts and Flowers*, and his travel book, *Sea and Sardinia*, which he dashed off in a few weeks after a visit to that island and, contrary to his usual habit, did not revise at all.

Fontana Vecchia had a superb situation. The dawn came up over the sea and the first sunshine poured into the bedroom. In the steep garden below their loggia there were the 'almond-trees beneath the terrace rail', to which one poem is directly addressed. He specially loved almond blossom. There were roses, too, and mimosa and mulberry-trees and a general luxuriance of vegetation. Close by were shimmering groves of olive and rich green, sweet-smelling rows of lemon-trees, and the

> Fig-trees, weird fig-trees
> Made of thick smooth silver,
> Made of sweet untarnished silver in the sea-southern air—

Along the stony track past their door the peasants passed singing on their donkeys, and the goatherds drove their pattering animals, playing reed pipes as they might have done in the time of Theocritus.

The Lawrences' life was, he wrote to Lady Cynthia Asquith, 'very easy, indolent, and devil-may-care'. Frieda recalled those happy days long afterwards. 'We lived the rhythm of a simple life.' They rose early. Lawrence wrote or helped in the house, washing up, cleaning the floor, picking tangerines or fetching water from the trough. It was there that he met a snake drinking and stood patiently waiting in his pyjamas, pitcher in hand, till his dangerous guest slid away. This was the incident that inspired one of his best-known poems.

A sly old Sicilian woman, Grazia, did their shopping and Lawrence always went over the accounts with her. 'She can rook me a little, but not too much,' he told Frieda good-humouredly. Most days they cooked on charcoal fires, but on Sundays he lit the big kitchen stove. Frieda, under his tuition, had become more interested in household skills. She made cakes and tarts of all kinds, fruit-pies and meat-pies. They used to set them all out on the dining-room sideboard and call them 'Mrs Beeton's show'.

Lawrence preferred this quiet, private existence to the gossipy little world of Capri. He did not mind people as such, but he was happier with ordinary folk who knew nothing of his books and did not want to talk about them. Only Frieda read his new work, daily, as he set it down on paper. She had to understand what he was doing and approve of it. Hers was the opinion that mattered to him. Sometimes she preferred the first draft, regretted the incessant revision. But Lawrence must do as he thought fit.

Her task was to protect the wavering flame of his genius. Ever at the back of her mind she was aware of his physical fragility, so different from her own strength. Twice, before she knew him, he had nearly died. He caught cold so easily. All through their time together she lived with the secret fear, not to be shared with him, that he would be taken from her.

Things were better in Sicily. It was not only the kinder climate. In those miserable war years in England she had been able to do so little for him, she had felt sometimes more of a millstone round his neck. At Taormina she could make a home for him, help him to do the work he had to do.

Their quiet existence was varied with visitors and expeditions of their own, to Syracuse, to Malta, to the

Italian mainland. They went to Germany too.

Frieda's mother was living at the once-fashionable spa of Baden-Baden in a kind of home for widows of distinguished men. She had completely accepted the man who had brought her daughter so much turmoil and hardship. She knew that their happiness had more than made up for everything. 'It's strange,' she told Frieda, 'that an old woman can still be as fond of a man as I am of that Lorenzo.' She knew the importance of Frieda to his work. 'It's always you in Lorenzo's books. All his women are you.' She was nervous lest the other genteel old ladies should read those books, but no breath of scandal seemed to reach them. Lawrence was always on his best behaviour when visiting the Baroness, and as he was clearly a man of education they played for safety and called him 'Herr Doktor'. Much of his *Fantasia of the Unconscious* was written in the pinewoods close by.

They stayed also with Frieda's sister, Nusch. The charming, impulsive Nusch could take liberties with him that no one else dared. Nusch would fling herself into his lap like a kitten, crying out in her broken English, 'O Lorenzo, you are so nice – I like your red beard!' He was mostly called, now, by the Italian form of his name.

The Baroness might fear for what the other old ladies would say if they read his books and even Lady Cynthia might hint that he had a bee in his bonnet about sex, but others welcomed his frankness. The world was in a mental ferment after the war. Just as, in politics, the Russian Communists had overthrown the established order, and in Italy and Germany Mussolini and Hitler were beginning their attack on Western democracy, so too, in the sphere of individual behaviour – sex, marriage, education – the old standards were being assailed. The 'permissive society' of the nineteen-seventies grew from seeds scattered in the nineteen-twenties. Books and plays would still be banned, men and women persecuted for their moral views and private actions, but there would be no return to Victorian stuffiness. When *The Rainbow* was republished, the police took no action.

Rolf Gardiner, an idealistic poet and reformer who later had a distinguished public career, was barely twenty at this time. 'Lawrence,' he was to declare, 'became the torchbearer, the torch leader of my youth. He went ahead exploring the dark.'

Very similar is the tribute of Rhys Davies, the Welsh novelist: 'For the younger generation of writers in England then, in that strange confused directionless decade after the war, he alone seemed to be carrying a torch. True, a smoky, wild torch. But nevertheless a light.'

Lawrence knew what he was doing. When he met Rhys Davies in 1928 he told him bluntly: 'All you young writers have me to thank for what freedom you enjoy. It was I who set about smashing down the barriers.'

Frieda might have been happy for ever at 'our beloved Fontana Vecchia', but in Lawrence the demon of restlessness was soon astir again. He complained of the weather even in Sicily, sometimes 'monstrous hot', sometimes 'deadly cold and horrid' with January thunderstorms and hail. 'The south is so lifeless,' he wrote to Eleanor Farjeon. 'There's ten times more "go" in Tuscany.' Malta was worse than Sicily: the British atmosphere and influence set him on edge. He had liked Sardinia, but there was 'no point in living there'. He would have loved France – 'without the French'. The Italians had changed since the war and were nowadays 'really rather low-bred swine'.

In short, Lawrence was becoming increasingly misanthropic, a remarkable development for a man who, however ill-used he had sometimes been, was rich in friends and well-wishers. He liked people better at a distance. In letters his warmth was undiminished. Confronted with friends at close quarters, he quickly tired of them and was apt to quarrel. His changes were abrupt. He, with his faith in 'instinct' and 'blood', was not interested in logic or consistency. Almost every opinion he threw off, in one mood, can be contradicted by what he said or wrote in another. Quotations from Lawrence can be dangerously misleading.

As with persons, so with places. The distant, and especially the yet-unknown, always seemed more attractive. In 1921 he was in the mood to condemn all Europe and to build hopes on the continents he had never seen. America had long attracted him. There had been the foredoomed wartime plan to settle in Florida. Now he began to hanker after 'a little farm somewhere by myself in Mexico or British Columbia'. For some years, off and on, he had been working at essays on Fenimore Cooper, Herman Melville, and other authors, which he published in 1923 as *Studies in Classic American Literature*. Even more was he drawn to the idea of the old America that had preceded the white man. Perhaps the surviving Red Indians retained the primitive wisdom of the blood which civilization had destroyed elsewhere?

By coincidence he had now received a letter from an American reader, Mrs Mabel Dodge Sterne, urging him to come and settle on her estate at Taos in New Mexico, in the midst of those same Red Indians.

Mrs Sterne was a remarkable character, well worth her place in the gallery of women who figured in Lawrence's life.

She was then forty-three, the same age as Frieda. She had divorced her third husband, a painter, and was soon to marry her Indian chauffeur and already close companion, Tony Luhan. She was wealthy and had already treated herself to a course of the newly fashionable psychoanalysis. She saw herself as a patron of writers and artists and as a Lady Bountiful to the Indians who farmed the land around her comfortable home. After reading *Sea and Sardinia* she thought what a wonderful thing it would be to lure this young English author to Taos so that he would write about her beloved Indians.

A correspondence developed, but with no air mail across the Atlantic this was sometimes too slow for Mrs Sterne's impulsive nature. She sent cables to reinforce her letters. And, being of a mystical nature too, each night as she lay down to sleep she willed him to come. Tony, the chauffeur, had to co-operate in radiating these thought-waves, and did so without undue enthusiasm. His mistress was a woman who liked her own way.

The transmission was not an immediate success. Lawrence was uneasy. Would he find Taos to be one of those 'arty' colonies he hated? Could he afford it? Mrs Sterne was offering a cottage, but did her generosity go further? His income was still small and uncertain.

He had, however, reached the brink of acceptance at the beginning of 1922. 'We had almost booked our passage to America when suddenly it came over me, I must go to Ceylon.' Sadly, in February, Frieda began to pack once more.

Why Ceylon? There too Lawrence had American friends offering him hospitality. Mr and Mrs Earl Brewster were a well-to-do couple, interested in painting and Buddhism. Lawrence had no sympathy with the 'inaction and meditation' involved in that religion, but in his disgust with the western civilization he declared that Buddhistic peace was 'the point to start from, not our strident fretting and squabbling.'

They sailed from Naples in a liner bound for Australia and he enjoyed the voyage. It began well when they found themselves sharing a table with a Mrs Jenkins returning to Perth. She was a keen novel-reader and let fall mention of *Sons and Lovers* which enabled Frieda to say, 'Oh, that's my husband's book.' They made friends with her and other passengers. Lawrence was well and in good humour.

In letters to friends – and no one has ever written better descriptive letters than he did throughout his life – Lawrence sketched the landmarks of their journey. 'We saw our Etna like a white queen ... standing in the sky so magic lovely.' They crept through the Suez Canal at five miles an hour, giving ample leisure to study life along its banks. They saw sunset over the Egyptian desert, 'a sky like a sword burning green and pink ... one felt near to the doors of the old Paradise.' To port they viewed Mount Sinai, 'red like old dried blood, naked like a knife and so sharp'. Emerging into the Indian Ocean, they were diverted by flying-fish, like silver butterflies, and the 'little black dolphins ... like little black pigs'.

In Ceylon, however, Lawrence wilted in the extreme heat. They went to the Brewsters' spacious bungalow on the hill above Kandy. There was 'jungle round the house, palms and noisy, scraping and squeaking tropical creatures; good-looking, more-or-less naked, dark bluey-brown natives'. There were coconut and cocoa plantations all around, the place was beautiful with 'such sweet scents', but he felt that he did not belong there and never would. Apart from his poem, 'Elephant', he wrote nothing about Ceylon.

Illness threw him into a homesick mood. He considered a return to England. 'I do think,' he wrote, 'that we make a mistake forsaking England ...' In this frame of mind he declared that 'the most living clue of life is in us Englishmen in England ... It is in ourselves or nowhere, and this looking to the outer masses is only a betrayal.' Such inconsistencies were characteristic. They were the price to be paid for basing statements on the prompting of his blood rather than his brain.

After six weeks they sailed on. They landed for a while in Western Australia, where Mrs Jenkins and her friends gave them a cordial welcome, including a barbecue on the hills overlooking the Swan River, with the 'billy' boiling water for tea and chops grilling over the wood fire. They then embarked again for Sydney. They rented a bungalow named 'Wyewurk' at Thirroul, forty miles south along the coast, and once more Frieda tried to create a home. At first – as usual – Lawrence liked the new place and was full of praise for it.

He liked the country but not the people. They were friendly, but he could not talk to them. If he lived there all his life, he felt, he would never know anybody. He clearly resented their healthiness and their materialism. They were always 'vaguely and meaninglessly on the go', to his thinking 'almost imbecile'. That was what life did to you in a new country, it made you 'so *outward*, that your real inner life and your inner self dies out, and you clatter round like so many mechanical animals.' It was the most democratic place he had ever been in, and the more he saw of democracy the more he disliked it.

In the landscape, though, he found great fascination, 'a sort of lure in the bush'. It was such a 'weird, big country ... so empty and untrodden.' But if he stayed, he told Mrs Brewster, he would 'really go bush'. It was 'just a bit too soon' to drop out. 'There is still some fight to fight, I suppose.'

In six weeks he almost completed a novel, *Kangaroo*, a book strong on description and atmosphere, as might be expected, but showing no deep understanding of the Australian people. Then, though Frieda would have been happy to stay, she had to pack again. They were to sail, via New Zealand and Tahiti, across the Pacific to San Francisco, taking up Mrs Sterne's invitation to New Mexico.

The old Baroness had written to her beloved son-in-law, betraying a little vexation at the way he was dragging Frieda from continent to continent. 'I tell you again,' he retorted, 'the world is round and brings the rolling stone home again. And I must go on till I find something that gives me peace.'

They reached San Francisco early in September, land-sick after almost a month of shifting decks underfoot. A warmly welcoming message from Mrs Sterne awaited them: from this point they were her guests and she sent the rail tickets. When they stepped down after their two-day journey through the desert, there she was, a masterful little woman in a turquoise blue dress with Indian jewellery. Beside her stood a burly Indian, his blanket girded with a massive silver belt – Tony. The effort to 'will' Lawrence across the world had succeeded. What now?

They drove next morning through the deep canyon of the Rio Grande and up to Taos, an oasis seven thousand feet up amid the sage desert, with higher dark blue peaks clustered in a distant crescent. The adobe houses were golden in the sun. Golden too were the autumn-tinted poplars and cottontrees, golden the stubble fields of the neighbouring Indian reservation.

Mabel Sterne had built them a cottage on her land, a four-roomed adobe building, bright with rugs and furniture of Mexican or Navajo Indian workmanship. The guests were to be independent, Lawrence's genius was to flower free from interruption. Such was the theory.

Mabel, however, had come to the conclusion that Lawrence's genius needed powering by a woman like herself. Nothing so crude as a love-affair was in her mind, although, if it was true that the body was the gateway to the soul, she was prepared for anything necessary to the task she had undertaken. To begin with, she suggested that Lawrence should help her with a book on her most interesting life. It was hard for him to refuse. Soon he had to tell her, 'Frieda thinks we ought to work in *our* house.'

'With *her* there?' said Mabel, too aghast to be subtle.

'Well –' Lawrence hesitated. 'Not in the room – all the time. She has her work to do.'

Mabel knew she was beaten. In her own version of the affair – for of course she too wrote a book afterwards, *Lorenzo in Taos* – she says: 'I should never have the opportunity to get at him and give him what I thought he needed, or have, myself, the chance to unload my accumulation of power.'

On another occasion Lawrence gave her a plain hint. They were washing dishes and their fingers touched under the soapsuds. Lawrence exclaimed – and according to Mabel's lush description he did so 'with a blue and gold look' (whatever that was) 'through the clamour of the magnetic bells':

'There is something more important than love!'

'What?' asked Mabel.

And he told her, grimly, 'Fidelity!'

Mabel was a difficult hostess to be obliged to. One day she marched over to the Lawrences' cottage and upset Frieda by telling her she was not the right woman for Lorenzo. Frieda flared up.

'Try it yourself, then, living with a genius! See what it's like and how easy it is. Take him if you can.'

In December the Lawrences thanked Mabel and removed themselves to an old log cabin they rented on the Del Monte Ranch, seventeen miles away. 'Mabel was too near a neighbour,' he wrote to a friend, and to the Baroness he explained that they were not taking 'this snake to our bosom'. There were too many supper-parties and drives and people dropping in.

They felt freer and happier on the ranch, but were saddened to hear, early in the new year, that Katherine Mansfield had died in France after a long struggle against tuberculosis. The gay young New Zealander had been

135

only thirty-three, but her short stories had already earned her a place in literature. Lawrence's letter of sympathy to Murry was full of forebodings. He had the sense that 'old moorings were breaking'. What was going to happen to them all? But, he said, 'The dead don't die. They look on and help.' He looked forward to seeing Murry again when he went to England. It had been 'a savage enough pilgrimage these last four years.'

New Mexico, needless to say, was not going to be the end of that pilgrimage. He found interest in the Indians, their dances and ceremonies, the primitive beliefs oddly veneered over with Catholic teaching – the Virgin's statue paraded to a mingled accompaniment of hymn-singing and war-whoops, and clearly regarded more as the Goddess of the Harvest than as the mother of Jesus. But he could not make real contact with the Indians, they were 'much more remote than negroes'. To that extent, New Mexico was no answer to anything.

Otherwise, life could be pleasant enough. He took up riding. He was completely new to it, and his posture would have horrified a riding-master, but, Mabel test-ified, 'he was absolutely fearless and never fell off, no matter what the horse did.' He would ride his little mare at breakneck speed, oddly hunched up in the saddle, leaning forward eagerly, or standing up in the stirrups. He could be seen most afternoons, a flat white hat cram-med on his head, a white woollen jacket over his blue sweater, with Frieda galloping behind him in trousers and a loose embroidered smock. She was 'terribly happy, feeling the live horse under me'. Lawrence teased her: 'If only you were as nice with me as you are with Azul!'

They remained outwardly friends with Mabel and had plenty of other friends too. Lawrence was feeling more sociable than he had been in Australia. There were flashes of the old Lawrence. He got them all acting charades.

He convulsed his American guests with stories and imitations of the English celebrities he had known. He paced the room, 'taking the part first of the Countess and then of the Cabinet Minister', till he collapsed overcome with laughter. An objective observer, the American painter Andrew Dasburg, declared that 'he was one of the most lovable human beings I have ever known, gentle as well as radiant with inner happiness.' But the give-and-take of quiet conversation was not his strong point. He was too much like an evangelist. One had to listen to *him*, eloquently explaining, violently denouncing.

After some months at their log cabin the Lawrences paid a lengthy visit to the republic of Mexico across the border. Lawrence stormed out of a bull-fight in disgust, but he was fascinated by the pyramids and other impressive relics of the Aztecs. He was specially attracted by the legends of the fair-skinned hero-god, Quetzalcoatl, and began rapidly writing a novel with that title, later changed to *The Plumed Serpent*. For this period they settled in the lakeside village of Chapala. Every day he sat under the trees, covering page after page of a thick blue notebook, raising his eyes at intervals to gaze at the fishermen, the dark-headed little boys hawking curios and the women doing their laundry in the chalky water.

Frieda wanted to see her children, now grown up. Lawrence took her by train across Texas, then by ship from New Orleans to New York, and saw her off to England. He returned alone to Mexico, via Los Angeles. Arrived in London, Frieda took a small flat in Hampstead to be near her children. But, having lived without a mother for eleven years, the young people (however affectionate) could hardly be expected to spend all their time with her, and Frieda had to repair the friendships weakened by long absence abroad. One, naturally, was Murry, who was editing a magazine, *The Adelphi*, which he had founded as a platform for Lawrence's ideas. He still considered himself Lawrence's loyal disciple and wanted him to come back and take over the paper, but Lawrence was unwilling to become involved.

Frieda and Murry were both lonely. Katherine Mansfield had died only in the January of that year. Frieda was going through a crisis in her relations with Lawrence. He had declined to accompany her to England. Probably the physical side of their marriage was diminishing, through his intermittent poor health, for within another year or two she was confiding to intimate friends that he could no longer make love to her, a fact which must have produced a profound effect on a woman with her passionate instincts. Even in that autumn of 1923 the loneliness and separation caused a flare-up of feeling between Murry and herself. Frieda was ready for a love-affair. Murry, though equally stirred, refused to betray Lawrence. So nothing happened, except that Frieda cabled her husband, renewing her plea that he should join her in London. At the end of November he sailed.

The next three months were full ones. He spent Christmas with his sisters and then went with Frieda to see her mother in Germany, pausing both ways in Paris, 'rather lovely in sunshine and frost ... but all like a museum.' He complained that he could no longer respond to Europe. Of the two continents America still offered him more promise. Hence the famous 'Last Supper' scene – no one could avoid seeing it in Biblical terms – when he gave a party for his oldest friends and admirers.

For this purpose he hired a private room at the Café Royal, facing Piccadilly Circus, which had been since Oscar Wilde's time the acknowledged rendezvous for men-of-letters. A coal fire blazed in the grate, all was gilt and red plush and flashing mirrors in the ornate late-Victorian manner. Frieda and Lawrence had collected seven guests round the circular table, and as several have left accounts of the evening it is possible to reconstruct most of the details.

On Lawrence's left sat the Hon. Dorothy Brett, a viscount's daughter and an artist, young, not unattractive, but shy and tragically afflicted by deafness, which at that date she could only alleviate by using a conspicuous ear-trumpet. 'Brett', as they called her, adored Lawrence and accepted his lightest word as gospel. Frieda longed for Brett to contradict him, but she never would.

Then, clockwise round the supper-table, there were Murry, Frieda, and Catherine Carswell, a Glasgow novelist who was to write a book on Lawrence, *The Savage Pilgrimage*. Then came the artist, Mark Gertler, Catherine's journalist husband, Donald, Koteliansky, dark-suited and sombre, and finally Mary Cannan, petite and beautiful as the heroine of any romantic novel, wearing a black silk evening dress and – oddly for such an occasion – a large picture-hat.

It was a good meal, worthy of that famous restaurant, but as a convivial occasion it was slow to warm up. There were undercurrents. Some of the guests were united only in their friendship with Lawrence. Jealousies and dislikes divided them. Conversation limped. But as the waiter moved round with the claret, refilling their glasses, the party slowly came to life. Lawrence tried hard to play the good host, a conventional role to which he was not accustomed. A very moderate drinker himself, he encouraged them to take more claret. At the end of the meal he tried to avoid offering port, because it always disagreed with him, but some of the men overruled him, insisting that it was the proper wine with which to round off the feast.

Things were going better now. The waiters had withdrawn, there was warmth and intimacy, the emotional temperature was rising. Koteliansky rose, pushed back his chair, and let loose a flow of Slavonic eloquence.

'Lawrence is a great man,' he declared. With a theatrical gesture he smashed a wine-glass to emphasise his point. He continued in the same manner, voluble, with flashing eyes and waving hands. 'Nobody here realises how great he is.' He broke a second wine-glass to prove it. 'Especially no woman, here or anywhere, can possibly realise the greatness of Lawrence.' Another glass went. 'Frieda does not count, Frieda is different,' he added handsomely, remembering his hostess. 'I understand and do not include her. But no other woman –' he glared round at Catherine and Mary and poor Brett, straining to hear through her ear-trumpet – 'no other woman can understand anything about Lawrence or what kind of being he is.' He sacrificed another glass in tribute to the genius.

Lawrence also made a speech. Disappointed with Europe, eager to return to Mexico, he sketched his old dream of forming a like-minded group to escape together from materialistic civilization. He threw out a challenging invitation. Would they go back to Mexico with him and build a new life?

This was something very different from rhetorical phrases. Koteliansky made a polite but unconvincing response. So did Gertler and Donald Carswell. Catherine Carswell said 'yes' with more enthusiasm, but could not imagine in her heart how it would be possible.

Mary Cannan was honest. 'No,' she said. 'I like you, Lawrence, but not so much as all that. I think you're asking what no human being has a right to ask of another.'

Lawrence asked Brett. 'Will *you* come with me, or would you be afraid?'

'No, I wouldn't be afraid. I'll go anywhere with you.'

Murry came round the table and sentimentally, in conscious imitation of Judas, kissed him and declared, 'I love you, Lorenzo, but I won't promise not to betray you.'

It was getting late. Mary made her excuses and left in good order. Gertler went too. Then the port, which Lawrence should never have drunk, took effect with undignified results and he was sick over the table. The ever-faithful Brett comforted him. Frieda stood aloof and furious, an outraged Wagnerian goddess. A taxi was ordered to transport Lawrence, half-conscious and collapsed, to the flat in Hampstead. Carswell, the hard-headed Scottish journalist, being the soberest of the men, settled the bill which he found was surprisingly reasonable, considering the mess and breakages.

In March the Lawrences, with Brett in tow, went back to Taos. Mabel, now married to Tony Luhan, had previously made Frieda the gift of a little ranch not far away. Lawrence was reluctant to accept such generosity from any one, but consented when Frieda gave Mabel the original manuscript of *Sons and Lovers* in exchange.

The ranch was a run-down place. With three Indians and a Mexican carpenter they worked hard to restore it. Lawrence was up at five each morning. Brett, more accustomed to an artist's studio, slaved at heavy manual tasks. Frieda 'cooked huge meals for everybody'. They had four horses, a black cow called Susan, a beautiful cockerel, Moses, and a flock of white hens. This was the ranch depicted in the novel, *St Mawr*, written at this time.

It was a prolific period in Lawrence's life. The three years in America produced also *The Plumed Serpent*, a travel book, *Mornings in Mexico*, a play, *David*, and much more. Mabel was herself *The Woman Who Rode Away*.

'I do like having the big, unbroken spaces round me,'

141

Lawrence wrote to Catherine Carswell. But the altitude, 8,600 feet, was bad for his chest. In October they went south for the winter, to Mexico City and Oaxaca. Brett went with them. Frieda was getting very tired of Brett – and of Tony – but Lawrence found her useful for typing his books.

In February he fell ill. Frieda was seized with forebodings. She feared that this time he was doomed, that he would never be really well again, and that all her love and strength could not restore him. The doctors in Mexico City told her to take him back to the ranch. It was the only hope. He had tuberculosis in the third degree. 'A year or two at the most,' they warned her.

It looked as if they had been unduly pessimistic. Back at the ranch, Lawrence gained strength, though he did no farm jobs beyond milking the cow and irrigating the field. He could ride, though, and do some writing. He never spoke of tuberculosis, but referred to his illness as influenza followed by malaria.

The old discontent was on him again. Despite all he had said about Europe the previous year he was hankering to return. 'I don't feel myself very American,' he wrote to the Baroness, 'no, I am still a European.' He felt it almost impossible, he told a friend, to be a purely creative writer in the United States. 'Everybody compromises with journalism and commerce.' America esteemed journalism. 'It loves a thrill or a sensation, but loathes to be in any way *moved*, inwardly affected so that a new vital adjustment is necessary.' Americans might be 'enormously adaptable' but they could not adjust themselves 'vitally, inwardly, to a rather scaring world, and at the same time get ahead.' Half a century later, after the Depression, World War Two, the invention of the atom bomb, the Vietnam war, and other traumatic shocks to the American system, he would have found much sympathy for such anti-materialist views, especially among the disenchanted young. At the time, however, he was voicing heresy.

In September, 1925, the Lawrences sailed from New York for Southampton, just three years after their first arrival in San Francisco.

The rolling stone was back – for the moment. Lawrence was seen in London again, frail and distinguished-looking in a black suit, his face 'pinched and small' under a wide-brimmed Mexican hat. He was just forty, but there was already a glint of silver in the hair at his temples.

He was now one of the three British novelists most influencing the taste of the intelligent reading public. The others were the satirical Aldous Huxley, who increasingly became his close friend, and Virginia Woolf, who used the 'stream of consciousness' technique devised by James Joyce in *Ulysses*. Joyce himself was not at this date so well known to the public, for *Ulysses* had been banned in both Britain and America.

Lawrence was thus 'established', and either famous or notorious, revered or detested, according to the prejudices of the individual. Libraries still looked askance at his novels, but his sales were sufficient to guarantee some degree of financial security, and he was able to send welcome little sums, as well as carefully made-up parcels, to the old Baroness in her genteel rest-home. But, as too often happens with authors, what Lawrence's books brought him in his lifetime was nothing to the shower of gold which descended on his grave when it was too late for him to benefit.

At least he could live where he liked, travel when he wished, and work in his own time. His needs were few, his tastes not luxurious.

He visited his sisters, saw Eastwood again, and came sadly away. Town and countryside had decayed since his boyhood. Eastwood had more than its share of the million and a quarter unemployed in Britain. The miners faced pay-cuts that were soon to force the long lock-out and the General Strike of 1926. 'I can't look at the body of my past,' said Lawrence. 'The spirit seems to have flown.' More than ever he felt that industrialism had poisoned the roots of human life.

The Lawrences went to Italy again. First they took the Villa Bernarda at Spotorno on the hilly coast near Genoa. Terms were quickly settled with the owner, Angelo Ravagli, a man after Frieda's own heart, as became apparent many years later. At their original interview Ravagli was resplendent in his dress uniform as a lieutenant in the famous mountain regiment, the Bersaglieri, with blue sash and jauntily tilted hat with cock feathers.

Now, to her joy, Frieda could invite her daughters to stay. Lawrence got on well with Elsa and Barby, but was jealous of them. Inclined as he was to instinctive rather than rational behaviour, he sometimes acted abominably.

'Don't imagine your mother loves you,' he warned Barby. 'She doesn't love anybody. Look at her false face!' And into that face he threw half a glassful of red wine.

The girl leapt to her feet. 'My mother's too good for you, much too good! It's like pearls before swine.' She burst into tears, and so did Frieda, rushing from the room.

Lawrence invited his sister Ada to come out and bring a woman friend. Between Ada and Frieda there had always been war. Ada had never forgiven the scandal of the divorce. 'I hate you from the bottom of my heart,' she told her hostess.

The villa was too small to hold them all in this mood. Lawrence went off with Ada and her friend, Frieda remained with her daughters. Lawrence joined the Brewsters, now in Capri. As a peace-offering he sent Frieda a picture of Jonah confronting the whale, with the caption, 'Who is going to swallow whom?'

Elsa and Barby talked their mother round. 'Now, Mrs L.,' they lectured her, 'be reasonable. You've married him. Now you must stick to him.' They all three went to the station to welcome him back. 'Make yourself look nice to meet him,' the girls insisted, and she obeyed.

Lawrence and Frieda needed no third party to detonate these explosive rows between them. They could quarrel about anything, and did. Lawrence would criticise her for smoking too many cigarettes, eating too many cakes, having her hair cropped, or expressing any opinion of which (at that moment) he disapproved. One day, in company, she was hotly denouncing the activities of the newspaper-owner, Lord Beaverbrook. Lawrence, himself calm for once, reproved her.

'Not so much intensity, Frieda.'

Frieda exploded. 'If I want to be intense, I'll *be* intense. And you go to hell.'

She was no Brett, to be walked over. Frieda could stand up for herself. But such quarrels, often gleefully retailed by other witnesses, implied nothing deeply wrong with their relationship, only the passion of their two natures. That Frieda, with all her spirit and vitality, stuck to her ailing, infuriating husband through everything, is the measure of the bond between them.

After a while they moved to Tuscany. Frieda fell in love at first sight with the Villa Mirenda, standing on a hill overlooking the Arno valley. Florence was a half-hour's tram-ride away. Lawrence never learned to drive a car. He would travel in a friend's, but he regarded the automobile as another example of the mechanization that was spoiling life.

There were few other English people in the area. He did not mind that. He made friends with the villagers. His Italian had become quite fluent, and he was soon a familiar and popular figure in his panama hat and bright blue linen jacket with enormous white buttons. He often carried a bag of boiled sweets in his pocket, and would even use one, however unsuitably, to comfort a child with toothache. For a boy more seriously ill, who required an operation, he paid the hospital bill in Florence. When the peasant women had babies, he would bear the cost of two-months' milk supply.

The Tuscan children had heard of a Christmas tree but had never seen one. Lawrence and Frieda ransacked the city shops for little wooden toys, wrapped up some sweets and dates, and hung them on a tree with candles and glittering decorations. Parents were invited too. In all, twenty-seven guests crowded into the room. There were glasses of wine for the elders, a long cigar for each of the men, biscuits for the women. It was quite an occasion.

Apart from such high days and holidays, life fell into a quiet routine. Lawrence rose early, as he always had done. After breakfast he might walk down, basket in hand, to do the shopping in the village. He still did much of the housework, cooking, ironing, mending his own shirts, and battling with an obstinate kitchen-stove which sent out clouds of suffocating smoke. He loved working with his hands, even to embroidery and the weaving of straw hats. When some English friends rented a house near by, he scrubbed the floors, cleaned the windows, and washed down the walls and paintwork before they arrived. To be Lawrence's friend was always an interesting experience. He might behave like an angel or like a devil, but whatever the relationship it was a full-blooded one.

On mornings when there was no shopping he would wander into the woods of umbrella-pine, inhaling the resinous air, just as Mr Chambers had bidden him long ago at Haggs Farm. He might sit there, writing or reading. At this period he was studying the ancient Etruscans, whose mysterious tombs and relics were so plentifully scattered through the region. The resultant book, *Etruscan Places*, is rated by his biographer, Harry Moore, 'the most profound of his travel books'.

Before noon he would be back at the villa and the typewriter might be heard. He typed himself nowadays. In earlier days everything had gone down in exercise-books in his neat handwriting. Lunch was about one. Then he would take a brief siesta. If he was in the mood, the typing would start again. If he was not, he would read, do household chores, or paint.

Painting was beginning to interest him more and more. As a schoolboy and as a teacher he had been attracted to it. Many of his friends, Gertler and Brett and others, were artists. Barbara Weekley had been through art school, now, and her visits still further stimulated him. Being Lawrence, inevitably he had to tell her what to do, to deride her formal training and put her right.

'*Play* with the paint,' he told her. 'Forget all you learned at the art school.' And when her obedience pleased him, he encouraged her: 'It's good. There's air in it.'

Air ... vitality ... To painting he brought the same

attitude as he did to writing – a disregard for technique, an insistence on spontaneity.

His admirer, the young writer, Rhys Davies, says that Lawrence's own efforts 'were faulty in drawing and construction, bad pictures ... But because of that Lawrentian intensity in them the technical errors seemed not to matter.' Barby herself was well aware of his shortcomings but she acknowledged that his pictures were 'alive and mystical'. He often used his thumb instead of a brush, producing a shiny surface which reminded her of oleographs.

As in his writing, again, he was concerned with saying something – above all, something to shock the bourgeois public he saw as his enemies. He wanted to affirm the central importance in life of sex and to attack the old taboos and silences. Somewhere in each picture, he told Brewster, he deliberately included a male organ, to represent 'a deep, deep life which has been denied in us, and still is denied.' This was simply not permissible in the nineteen-twenties – fig-leaves were still in fashion. 'One would think,' Lawrence complained to his old Eastwood friend, Willie Hopkin, 'that the Almighty created us down to the waist and the Devil finished us off.'

It was in the same defiant spirit that he was using, in the novel he was then writing, the notorious 'four-letter words' which, though known to all if not spoken by all, were forbidden in print. This last novel, *Lady Chatterley's Lover*, was concerned with a passionate, unfulfilled woman, who, married to a husband disabled in the Great War, turned for satisfaction to his gamekeeper, one of those virile, primitive characters Lawrence liked to depict. He told Rhys Davies that he would write no more novels. This was to be his 'last attempt to tell men and women how to live.' He was getting tired of writing. Words bored him, he was more and more absorbed in his painting. It took less out of him. He talked to Barby of giving up being an author, and becoming a painter instead.

Opinions vary about the merits of *Lady Chatterley's Lover*. Some think it the best of his novels, others feel its message too strident, its technique too imperfect – and its deliberate, self-conscious obscenity too easy to parody. 'I always labour at the same thing,' Lawrence admitted, 'to make the sex relation valid and precious instead of shameful. And this novel is the furthest I've gone.'

On that point, at least, there was no disagreement. One typist threw up in disgust the task of making the final copies – his own amateurish typing was too slow. His friends, Catherine Carswell and Aldous Huxley's wife, Maria, finished the job between them. Clearly such a book could not be published in Britain or America at that time, though they might allow an expurgated version. The novel as originally written should be printed in Florence in a limited edition of a thousand signed copies and supplied by mail order. Many of these copies found their way discreetly into Britain, but it was not until thirty-two years later that the book became freely available there, and then only after a famous courtroom battle, far exceeding in publicity that of *The Rainbow* and with the opposite result.

Lawrence never saw the triumph of *Lady Chatterley*. In this closing phase of his life he had to endure another legal humiliation, this time over his pictures.

He was not particularly anxious to display them, much less sell any. He painted, he said, 'simply and solely for the fun of it'. In 1929, however, the year after the first publication of *Lady Chatterley's Lover*, he agreed to a show at the London gallery run by Mr and Mrs Philip Trotter. Not wishing to part with the paintings he put high prices on them to discourage buyers.

He did not himself go to England. His health was

becoming more precarious. He often thought wistfully of the New Mexico ranch, still Frieda's property, but he was afraid that the U.S. immigration authorities would not admit a person in his condition. It was best to spend most of each year somewhere near the Mediterranean and the hot summer months in the mountains, in Bavaria, Austria or Switzerland.

It was Frieda who went to London for the exhibition. It opened at the Warren Gallery in June. Though the pictures were deliberately marked at high prices a book of reproductions was on sale. The first two days passed without incident. Then the Sunday *Observer* printed an unfavourable notice, and soon the newspapers were in full cry.

'The human frame,' said the *Daily Express*, 'is shown in its most intimate details ... The subject will compel most spectators to recoil with horror.' There is in fact no evidence that visitors were seen staggering or showing signs of distress. The kind of art-lover who found his way to a one-man show in a private gallery was apt to be a mature and sophisticated person, more interested in painting than in pubic hair. Even Ada, who came down from Derbyshire to see her brother's pictures, viewed them with equanimity and defended them against their critics.

'A disgraceful exhibition,' thundered the *Daily Telegraph*. The *Daily Express* gave its readers an idea of what they might expect to see if they ventured inside the gallery. '"*Spring*", a study of six nude boys is revolting. "*Fight with an Amazon*", representing a hideous bearded man holding a fair-haired woman in his lascivious grip, while wolves with dripping jaws look on expectantly, is frankly indecent. "*Boccaccio Story*" is better not described.'

This publicity did not bring howling mobs to the gallery. The attendance was good, but not excessive: over

151

three weeks it averaged about seven hundred per day. Frieda was there a good deal, chatting to old friends, heartening every one with her high spirits. Her 'gusty visits', some one recalled, were like 'draughts of champagne'.

On July 4 the gallery put on a party in her honour, since the artist himself could not be there. Frieda rose to the occasion, donning red shoes and a colourful shawl, and beaming over the great sheaf of lilies with which she had been presented. This was the moment of triumph. The next day, the authorities struck.

Frieda was not at the gallery at the time. Mr and Mrs Trotter were finishing lunch when two police inspectors arrived. Stiffly they requested that the exhibition be closed 'forthwith', failing which proceedings would be taken against the organizers. The Trotters refused. Thereupon the police cordoned off the entrance and went round the gallery, deciding which of the pictures were obscene. Thirteen canvases were taken down and policemen carried them to a waiting van below. The two inspectors then examined some books that were on view. Four copies of Lawrence reproductions were seized, and they would have added a volume of Blake's, had they not been told that Blake was a famous artist who had been dead for more than a century. Another book aroused their worst suspicions since it appeared to be in the French language. The ensuing dialogue is on record.

'I have to ask you what this is, Mrs Trotter,' said Inspector Hester.

'It is a literal translation into French of *The Hunting of the Snark*.'

'But what is *The Hunting of the Snark*? I never heard of it.'

'Possibly not,' said Mrs Trotter dryly. 'It was written for children. By an English clergyman.'

'No need to be rude, madam,' said the inspector. But he gave Lewis Carroll the benefit of the doubt.

He left with the rest of the booty. Within the hour the evening newspaper placards were announcing the police-raid from the street-corners. Frieda, limping through the West End – she was under treatment for an injured ankle – had no mind for newspapers. The crowd on the pavement in front of the gallery had long dispersed, a flag still fluttered bravely outside bearing Lawrence's name. She entered, just before closing time, and the bare spaces on the walls were her first warning that something had happened.

There was nothing she could do. The pictures, she learned, were locked up in the cellar at Marlborough Street police-station – one could only hope that the cellar was dry. The case would not come before the magistrate for a month. She must return to Lawrence long before that.

Friends rallied round. She was particularly touched by the support of her three children. Even Monty, who did not know Lawrence nearly as well as the girls did, was entirely with them in defence of the pictures.

A telegram from Orioli, the Florentine publisher of *Lady Chatterley's Lover*, said that Lawrence was very ill. He had caught cold sitting on the beach. He made light of it afterwards, he was no stranger to these bouts, but the Italian was much distressed and afraid he might die. Frieda knew too much of Lawrence's worsening health to take any chances. She hurried back, found him recovered, and took him off to visit her mother at Baden-Baden.

As to the pictures, his main concern was to save them from destruction. He wrote to Mrs Trotter, instructing her to settle the case as best she could. He was not prepared to be a martyr in this matter and sacrifice his work just to make a propaganda point and campaign against the law. His pictures were 'sacred' to him. He would not 'have them burnt, for all the liberty of England.' He wanted 'no more crucifixions, no more martyrdoms.'

He was furiously angry, but he found relief in ridicule. It was then that he dashed off the poem, '1300 People' published in *Nettles* the next year:

> ... they stared and leered at the single spot
> where a figleaf might have been, and was not

But in his hands ridicule was not an effective weapon. He lacked the right kind of wit and humour, the control of his own power, so that his tone too easily became shrill and strained. Lawrence's scornful outbursts often seem petty and ignoble, though understandable as the utterances of a sick and much-tried man.

The case was tried by a magistrate of eighty-two, an age far beyond that at which magistrates are allowed to sit on the bench today. He did not order the destruction of the pictures, but they must not be shown again in public. On that condition they were returned to the gallery. Most of them eventually went to America, some being acquired as a tourist attraction by a hotel-proprietor at Taos, while others were bought by the University of Texas.

As in the *Rainbow* case, Lawrence himself had not been directly on trial. But again, as then, he had been pilloried in the eyes of the world as a purveyor of the obscene.

That autumn, 1929, he was forty-four.

He had produced, often literally with 'feverish' energy, an astounding body of work, as varied in form as it was in quality. It included a dozen novels, countless short stories, a thousand poems, essays, pamphlets, travel books, literary criticism and plays. Much was not published until after his death, and some of the rest reached only a fraction of the public that was to appreciate it later. In some fields, such as drama, his talents had gone completely unrecognized.

Even so, his was a name to conjure with. For a decade he had been the torchbearer to the rebellious young. Sometimes, as Rhys Davies had admitted, it had been a wild and smoky torch, but it had let light into dark places.

With Lawrence the torch was a favourite symbol and 'dark' was a favourite word. That September, in his

155

poem *Bavarian Gentians*, he wrote with the premonition of death:

> Reach me a gentian, give me a torch!
> let me guide myself with the blue, forked torch
>   of this flower
> down the darker and darker stairs, where blue
>   is darkened on blueness
> even where Persephone goes ...

The word 'torch' occurs six times in nineteen lines, 'dark' or its derivatives eighteen times.

It was four and a half years since the doctors in Mexico City had warned Frieda that he would live 'a year or two at the most'. They had been over-pessimistic, but the shadow was creeping forward.

One July afternoon at the villa in 1927 Lawrence came in from the garden and proudly showed Frieda the basket of fine peaches he had picked. He went to his room. Suddenly he called 'in a strange, gurgling voice'. She ran in. Blood was pouring from his mouth. She threw her arms round him, comforting him until the doctor came.

Lawrence referred to this and later attacks as 'bronchial haemorrhages'. The word 'tuberculosis' remained unspoken. But he was too widely read not to be reminded of that similar moment in the life of Keats. 'Bring me the candle,' Keats had said. And then he had added, 'I know the colour of that blood. It is arterial blood. That drop of blood is my death warrant.'

In the following June, 1928, they gave up the villa. Lawrence felt he would be better by the sea. Frieda sighed and began to pack. She had known such happy times there, apart from Lawrence's illnesses. But his health was all that mattered. She would go anywhere if it would prolong his life. The sympathetic peasants gathered mournfully to say goodbye and carried out their baggage. 'Like gnomes,' Frieda recalls, 'they crept under their loads down the path.'

They spent that winter at Richard Aldington's home on Port-Cros, an islet off the French coast near Toulon. They moved to the mainland, to Bandol. They tried Majorca – Lawrence was momentarily attracted to Spain but saw that Frieda would never take to the country and soon he agreed with her. 'The Spaniards have refused life so long,' he told Aldous Huxley in his usual sweeping way, 'that life now refuses them, and they are rancid.'

In October, 1929, they returned to Bandol, and took the Villa Beau Soleil, 'a sort of bungalow' (he described it), modern and easy to run, with a balcony overlooking the bay. When he woke at dawn he could watch the sunrise beyond the foot of the bed, and see the silhouettes of the fishermen standing up in their boats like mythological figures against the splendour of sea and sky. He liked Frieda to come in at that time. 'What kind of a night did you have?' she would ask anxiously, and he would answer, 'Not so bad,' but she felt he was only trying to comfort her. A little later, when he was too ill to pretend, he once said as she bade him good-night, 'Now I shall have to fight several battles of Waterloo before morning.'

Sometimes he felt strong enough to take short walks along the road, but even these meant painful effort of will-power. Frieda and he drew closer than ever before. His mind dwelt on the past. 'Why, oh why did we quarrel so much?' he asked her remorsefully. She could only answer, 'Such as we were, violent creatures, how could we help it?'

Old friends came to see them. The Brewsters took a house not far away. Lawrence entertained the Americans with gossipy anecdotes of his youth at Eastwood and with old dialect songs like *Turnip Hoeing* which he must once have sung at the Haggs. Frieda accompanied him on a little upright piano and he taught them all to sing the choruses.

He often thought of the farm. 'Whatever I forget, I shall never forget the Haggs,' he had written to David Chambers the year before. Did they still have stewed figs for tea in winter? Did his mother still blush if an unexpected visitor caught her in a dirty apron? 'Tell your mother I never forget, no matter where life carries us... Oh, I'd love to be nineteen again, and coming up through the Warren and catching the first glimpse of the buildings. Then I'd sit on the sofa under the window, and we'd crowd round the little table to tea, in that tiny little kitchen I was so at home in.'

He was reading Moffat's recently published translation of the Bible into modern English. A good book, he declared, should be translated afresh every ten years. 'I intend to find God,' he told Earl Brewster. 'I don't any longer object to the word God. My attitude has changed.' But he was not thinking solely of death. In some moods he talked eagerly of getting back to Frieda's ranch if only they would let him into the United States. 'I might perhaps get going with a few young people ... making a new concept of life. Who knows?' He dreamed of a 'school, like the Greek philosophers', walking and talking under the pine-trees in New Mexico.

Christmas was gay. His sisters sent two hampers full of traditional English fare, plum pudding, mincemeat and Christmas cake. Lawrence himself felt well enough to make lemon tarts.

In January he was visited by an English doctor on holiday. Mark Gertler had staged the meeting as tactfully as he could, knowing Lawrence's resistance to doctors and all the varied treatments he had been given in different places without success. With Dr Morland he got on quite well. Morland was impressed by Lawrence's remarkable survival after so many years of doing all the wrong things. He recognized that the very qualities which helped to make Lawrence a genius tended also to prevent his keeping to the quiet, sensible routine his illness demanded. If only Lawrence would *rest*! But that was the one thing, in all his tumultuous vagrant life he had never learned to do.

The doctor achieved one unlikely success: he persuaded Lawrence, who hated the very idea of a sanatorium, to enter one, the Ad Astra, at Vence further along the mountainous coast towards Italy. Lawrence was still talking of the ranch. 'I believe I *should* get strong if I could get back.' As always he clung to the illusion that some other place would be better than the one where he was. Guardedly the doctor said that, with two months' absolute rest, he might be fit to travel. Lawrence, he thought privately, had still a slender chance. The case was not hopeless.

'The almond trees are all in blossom,' Lawrence wrote from Bandol at the end of January, 'but I am not allowed any more to go out and see them.' The sun was brilliant, the sea dazzling blue with white foam, but an icy wind, the mistral, was blowing down from the Alps. He lay in the sheltered entrance of the garage.

He saw plenty of almond blossom a week later, when they took him along the coast to the sanatorium. He drove to the station in a car which Mrs Brewster had heaped with the delicate pink flowers. From the train he saw the clouds of blossom all the way to Antibes.

Vence was an ancient little town, a thousand feet up amid the Alpine foothills. The sanatorium was more like a guest-house, with a nurse taking temperatures and doctors looking in occasionally. He had an upstairs room with a balcony facing out over the distant Mediterranean. The room had yellow curtains and overpoweringly blue walls, but his friends countered the effect with masses of spring flowers. Brewster brought him books to read. His visitors included H. G. Wells and the Aga Khan. The American sculptor, Jo Davidson, turned up at Wells' suggestion and modelled his head as he sat on the balcony. Aldous and Maria Huxley, realising how ill he was, hurried from London, where they had been for the production of *This Way to Paradise*, a dramatization of Huxley's novel, *Point Counter Point*. In this the important character, Mark Rampion, represented Lawrence himself, while Murry appeared as 'Denis Burlap'.

Frieda, now supported by Barby, was staying not far from the sanatorium, but, since the nights were as usual the worst, she several times remained in the sick-room, sleeping on a cane chair. Once Lawrence, made irritable by his suffering, told her brusquely, 'Your sleeping here does me no good,' and she went out in tears, but when she came back he was tender again. 'You know I want nothing but you,' he said, 'but sometimes something is stronger in me.'

Within a week or two he decided that the sanatorium was no good. He insisted on leaving at the end of the month. Frieda found a villa to rent close by. An English nurse would come out from Nice. 'I shall be better looked after,' Lawrence assured her.

On March 1 they moved him to the villa by taxi. He was so weak now that he allowed Frieda to kneel and put on his shoes for him. The short drive exhausted him. He went to bed, and that night Frieda slept on a couch in his room. The next morning, a Sunday, he begged her not to leave him and she sat beside him, both of them reading. He ate lunch but during the afternoon began to feel very ill. His temperature was rising. He was in

160

pain and demanded an injection. Huxley hurried out in quest of a doctor to give it. 'Hold me,' Lawrence begged Frieda in delirium, 'I don't know where I am.'

The doctor came and gave the injection. Lawrence grew calmer. 'If only I could sweat,' he murmured, 'I would be better.' His breathing steadied. Frieda sat by the bed with Maria Huxley for company. 'I held his left ankle from time to time,' she recalled. 'It felt so full of life. All my life I shall hold his ankle in my hand.'

Towards ten o'clock the regular breathing became spasmodic. His chest heaved as he struggled for air. And then suddenly, unbelievably, it was all over, like the snapping of a thread. He was gone.

Two days later, on March 4 1930, he was buried in the small local graveyard. There was no service, just half a dozen friends kept Frieda and Barby company. 'Very simply, like a bird we put him away,' said Frieda afterwards, 'a few of us who loved him.' They heaped golden mimosa on the plain oak coffin. 'Good-bye, Lorenzo,' said Frieda as the earth was shovelled into the grave.

In due course the burial place was marked with Lawrence's favourite symbol, a phoenix, traced in coloured pebbles. It was a most fitting emblem. For just as, in the ancient Egyptian legend, a new phoenix was born from the funeral pyre of the old, so the immortal essence of Lawrence – the best of his work and his abiding message – took new life though the man himself was dead.

His influence, indirect as well as direct, has spread out since then in ever widening ripples. It is no exaggeration to say that, after Lawrence's novels, no serious novel written in English could be quite the same again, so that even people who never read a line of Lawrence's own work were to be affected at second and third hand. So too, even beyond the ranks of the book-readers, millions more would have their attitudes modified, though they might never know why, and might not even know the difference between D. H. Lawrence and Lawrence of Arabia. For D. H., more than any individual Englishman of his generation, had shed a light upon dark places and thrown down barriers that would not be put up again.

Those dark places, those barriers, were not solely concerned with sex, though it would be hard to overestimate the importance of his message, insisting that man's sexual life must be frank and joyful. To Lawrence, though, this was just part of something even greater and more fundamental, a reverence for life in all its manifestations. The flower, the insect, the tree, are all important. If there is triumph in the union of lovers there is tragedy in the pollution of a grass field in the name of industrial progress. This is a part of Lawrence's message more relevant today than ever before.

'We've got to live,' he wrote in the first paragraph of *Lady Chatterley's Lover*, 'no matter how many skies have fallen.' And the remedy for Man's troubles, Lawrence preached continually, lay within himself, in his own regeneration. Most of his intellectual contemporaries sought the remedy in political action, technical advances, better education, the welfare state. Lawrence felt that no material changes would, by themselves, improve the quality of life. He is seen now to have been right. But if his prophecies had been made in speeches or in academic books his name would barely have survived. It is because he poured out that volcanic flow of passionate poems, novels, stories, and the rest, that his thoughts remain, enshrined as though in the lava. So, in assessing his influence and appeal today, and his ultimate status as a writer it is impossible to separate the propagandist from the literary artist.

He had died young. For half a century afterwards

there would still be people alive who remembered him vividly – articulate people to write books and articles about him, humbler unknown people to be patiently traced by his biographers and questioned. That is why his life story can be reconstructed as vividly as a novel, with factual authority for every line of dialogue, every thought and sensation attributed to the characters.

What happened to the others – the few, especially, who had played leading roles in that story?

Jessie, who had become Mrs Wood, severed all connection with Lawrence after 1912 and in 1930 knew nothing of his illness or where he was. Yet on March 2, as she told Helen Corke in a letter, she had a distinct impression of hearing his voice saying suddenly, 'Can you remember only the pain and none of the joy?' The next morning, before the news of his death had broken in the English press, she had a vision of him as the schoolboy she had first met, his little High School cap on the back of his head. 'She was an intensely truthful woman,' Professor David Chambers testified in 1971, 'and I must accept this as a part of her experience.' His sister had died in 1944.

Louie Burrows had reacted quite differently from Jessie. She treasured all Lawrence's letters and twice visited his grave at Vence. 'One day,' Barby recalled, 'a tall dark woman came into the cemetery, but seeing us went away ... After we had left the cemetery, she came back and laid some flowers there.' She did not marry until ten years after that. She lived on until 1962.

And Frieda, the remarkable, irrepressible Frieda? She had been a good wife, she had stuck to Lawrence through eighteen years of storm and strain, she had shielded the flickering torch of genius until death quenched the last spark. She could do no more for him. At fifty she was still full of vitality.

Professor Weekley offered to let bygones be bygones. Would she return to Nottingham and become his wife once more? Frieda declined.

Murry and Lawrence had not been close in those final years. 'We belong to different worlds,' Lawrence had told him, 'different ways of consciousness.' But when Murry came out to visit his grave the old, once-suppressed attraction between him and Frieda erupted. There was now no practical impediment, for, though Murry had remarried after Katherine's death, he had lost his second wife too. He and Frieda became lovers, but the affair did not last. The next year, Murry published a book on Lawrence which so infuriated her that she solemnly burnt a copy and sent him the ashes. They remained friends, but stormily.

When she married again it was to Angelo Ravagli, whom she had first met, so dashing in his Bersaglieri uniform, when renting the villa near Genoa. They did not settle in Italy, but went to Frieda's ranch and lived there till her death, on her seventy-seventh birthday, August 11, 1956.

Lawrence, who had so longed to return to New Mexico during his final illness, was granted his desire in death. In 1935 his body was exhumed and cremated, so that the remains could be taken to Frieda at El Prado. The memorial phoenix of coloured pebbles did not cross the Atlantic, however – it found its way back to England and now has an honoured place on the panelled wall of the Council chamber in his native Eastwood.

Frieda built a little chapel near her home in New Mexico to house his ashes. There, cemented into the altar, so that they cannot easily be disturbed again, are the last earthly remains of that human phoenix, of whom she had once asked herself, long ago, *What kind of a bird is this?*

And by the chapel door, high in the Rockies on Lobo Mountain, Frieda herself now lies, his companion once more.

CHRONOLOGY OF LAWRENCE'S LIFE AND TIMES

1885 Lawrence born at Eastwood on September 11.

1893 Enters Beauvale School in that town.

1898 Wins scholarship to Nottingham High School.

1901 Death of Queen Victoria. Lawrence meets Jessie Chambers, takes first job as clerk, and has serious illness.

1902 Lawrence becomes a pupil-teacher.

1903 He meets Louise Burrows.

1906 Takes course at University College, Nottingham, and begins writing.

1908 Qualifies and takes a school post at Croydon, near London.

1909 Early work published in *The English Review*.

1910 December: engagement to Louie Burrows and death of his mother.

1911 January: publication of *The White Peacock*.
Katherine Mansfield's first book, *In A German Pension*.

Rupert Brooke's first poems and formation of the 'Georgian' group of poets. December: Lawrence very ill.

1912   Lawrence has to give up teaching. He breaks off his engagement to Louie, meets Frieda Weekley, and elopes with her. After Germany and Austria they settle at Gargnano on Lake Garda in Italy. Publication of *The Trespasser*.

1913   *Love Poems and Others* and *Sons and Lovers*. Compton Mackenzie's novel, *Sinister Street*, published.

1914   Return to England. Lawrence marries Frieda, July, and World War I breaks out in August. *The Prussian Officer and Other Stories*.

1915   *The Rainbow* is published and suppressed.

1917   *Amores* (poems) and *Twilight in Italy*.

1917   *Look! We Have Come Through!* (poems). The Lawrences expelled from Cornwall as suspected spies.

1918   Lawrence publishing only poems. The war ends with Germany's surrender on November 11.

1919   The Lawrences leave England in November and travel via Florence and Capri to Taormina.

1920   Publication of *Women in Love* and *The Lost Girl*. J. Middleton Murry's *Aspects of Literature*.

1921   *Psychoanalysis and the Unconscious*, *Tortoises* (poems), *Sea and Sardinia*, and (originally under a pen-name) *Movements in European History*. Aldous Huxley's novel, *Crome Yellow*.

1922   The Lawrences travel to New Mexico via Ceylon and Australia. *Aaron's Rod*, *Fantasia of the Unconscious*, and *England, My England* (short stories). Also published that year are Katherine Mansfield's *The Garden Party* and Virginia Woolf's first major work, *Jacob's Room*. James

Joyce's *Ulysses* is banned in Britain and the U.S.A. The B.B.C. begins public radio broadcasting in Britain.

1923 *Kangaroo, Birds, Beasts and Flowers* (poems), *The Ladybird* (stories) and *Studies in Classic American Literature*. The Lawrences visit Mexico and end the year in England. Katherine Mansfield dies in January. Murry founds and edits *The Adelphi*.

1924 Lawrences return to New Mexico. *The Boy in the Bush*. Murry edits *The Journal of Katherine Mansfield*.

1925 *St Mawr* and other stories. *Reflections on the Death of a Porcupine* (essay). Lawrence is ill, tuberculosis of the lungs is diagnosed, and he returns to Italy.

1926 *The Plumed Serpent*, various stories, and a play, *David*.

1927 *Mornings in Mexico*.

1928 *Lady Chatterley's Lover* published at Florence in its original limited edition. *The Woman Who Rode Away* (stories), The Lawrences leave their Tuscan villa and begin their final series of short stays at various places.

1929 *Pansies* (poems), *Pornography and Obscenity*, and other publications. London police seize Lawrence's paintings.

1930 Lawrence dies at Vence, in southern France, on March 2, leaving a great quantity of unpublished work which continues to appear for many years after his death.

SOME BOOKS FOR FURTHER READING

When first approaching D. H. Lawrence it is often better
to start with his shorter works. There are various collections of his verse, such as *D. H. Lawrence: Poems selected
for young people*, by William Cole, and *D. H. Lawrence:
Selected Poems*, with an introduction by W. E. Williams.
Similarly, there are *Selected Short Stories* and *Selected
Letters*. One volume in the Everyman Library, *Stories,
Essays, and Poems*, by D. H. Lawrence, edited with an
introduction by Desmond Hawkins, brings together a
wide variety of these shorter works.

Among the full-length novels one cannot do better
than begin with the classic *Sons and Lovers*, moving on
to the most important of his later work, *The Rainbow*
and its sequel, *Women in Love*. Those who particularly
appreciate the lyrical quality in *Sons and Lovers* will find
it well worth while to go back to his first book, *The
White Peacock*, which, though a less powerful story, has
much of the same quality. At the other end of the scale

comes the last novel of all, the famous (or notorious) *Lady Chatterley's Lover*, the literary merits of which have been hotly debated. Its importance as an influence on modern writing is undeniable, though most critics place it, technically, below the best of Lawrence. It is certainly not a sensible choice to begin with – it will be enjoyed and understood much better after a fair amount of his other fiction has been read.

Of books *about* Lawrence there are literally hundreds, some of them unsound and misleading, and only as one's knowledge extends can one learn to distinguish the truth from the prejudice. The standard full-length biography is Harry T. Moore's *The Intelligent Heart: The Story of D. H. Lawrence*. In the splendid three-volume *D. H. Lawrence: A Composite Biography* Edward Nehls has arranged, in chronological order, countless passages from Lawrence's own writings and from those who knew him at each stage of his life, so that he can be seen, 'in the round', against every background from Nottingham to New Mexico. Among the books quoted are many that the reader may wish to seek out and read in full. Notable are Jessie Chamber's memories, *D. H. Lawrence, A Personal Record* by 'E. T.', and Frieda Lawrence's *Not I, But the Wind*. . . . *Lawrence in Love: Letters from D. H. Lawrence to Louie Burrows*, edited by James T. Boulton, was published as late as 1968, so that its interesting material was not available when the earlier books appeared.

Index